Location of the area covered by this guide

HIGH SIERRA HIKING GUIDE

SILVER LAKE

The High Sierra between Carson Pass and Ebbetts Pass

Joseph R. Grodin
and Sharon Grodin

WILDERNESS PRESS
BERKELEY

First edition July 1976
Second edition March 1978
THIRD EDITION April 1983
Second printing April 1986
Third printing May 1988
Revised fourth printing April 1990
Fifth printing August 1992

Photos by Thomas Winnett (except frontispiece)
Design by Thomas Winnett
Cover design by Larry Van Dyke

Library of Congress Card Catalog Number 82-62832
International Standard Book Number 0-89997-027-3
Manufactured in the United States

Published by Wilderness Press
    2440 Bancroft Way
    Berkeley, CA 94704
    (510) 843-8080

Write for free catalog

Library of Congress Cataloging-in-Publication Data

Grodin, Joseph R.
  Silver Lake / by Joseph R. Grodin and Sharon Grodin.
    p.   cm. — (High Sierra hiking guide)
  Originally published: 3rd ed. Berkeley : Wilderness Press, 1983.
  Includes index.
  ISBN 0-89997-027-3
  1. Hiking—Sierra Nevada (Calif. and Nev.)—Guidebooks.
  2. Backpacking—Sierra Nevada (Calif. and Nev.)—Guidebooks.
  3. Sierra Nevada (Calif. and Nev.)—Guidebooks.   I. Grodin, Sharon.
  II. Title.   III. Series: High Sierra hiking guide (1986)
  GV199.42.S55G76 1992
  917.94'4—dc20   92-24782
                                         CIP

Preface

Writing this book has been a joyous experience, both for me and for my daughter Sharon, who assisted me—and not only because it provided an opportunity for our family to spend a summer together in one of our favorite areas after Sharon's first year in college. I am a lawyer and law teacher by profession; what I have written before has been about the law and social problems. I am also an avid hiker and backpacker, but my previous experience seldom forced me to view my physical surroundings with the same degree of attentiveness to detail that is required, say, to try a case in court or explain a complicated problem to a law class. This project forced me to do that, with the result that I, and Sharon as well, developed an increased awareness of our backpacking environment.

Ironically, that increased awareness led us to question the project itself. Parts of the area we describe are already overcrowded with campers during the summer. Other parts are remote, wild and seldom travelled, with trails ill-defined and unmapped. Were we, by calling further attention to the area, and by providing accurate maps and trail descriptions, contributing to the destruction of the very environment we had come to love and respect?

We finally resolved those doubts by a process of reasoning which the reader is free to call rationalization but which we accept as reasonably satisfying. First, it is likely that most people who would be induced to hike in "our" area by reason of this guide would otherwise be hiking somewhere else; and it would seem that the goal of environmental protection for wilderness areas is best served, or at least not adversely affected, by dispersion rather than by concentration.

Second, the notion of preserving "our" area for ourselves and others who happen to know about it has a selfish ring; if scarce resources are to be allocated (and wilderness areas are a scarce resource) keeping them secret does not seem the most equitable way to go about it.

Third, the business of protecting wilderness areas has a political dimension. The intrusion of loggers, jeepsters, motorcyclists, and even developers presents a much greater danger to the environment than do hikers and backpackers. To resist that kind of intrusion through proper governmental regulation requires a constituency, and that means people who know the area, love it, and are prepared to fight for it.

Where possible we have tailored available options toward the end of environmental protection. For example we encourage day trips rather than overnight stays in particularly tender areas. We refrain from describing the availability of wood in camping areas (please forgive us) in the hope that you will minimize your impact by bringing a stove. We call your attention to areas likely to be crowded, and to the rules of good campkeeping. And, rather than set forth "canned" trips, which tend to accentuate the use of "favorite" spots, we present open-ended descriptions of alternative routes in such a way as to enable you to decide for yourself whether a particular area sounds attractive, whether a trip is within the physical capabilities and the experience of you and your companions, and how to get where you want to go without losing your way, leaving to you the preparation of your own itinerary. We try not to intrude upon your perceptions, but we do call things to your attention from time to time, particularly matters of historical interest, which abound in the area and which happen to fascinate us.

Despite occasional overuse the area remains one of the loveliest and most unspoiled in the entire Sierra Nevada. Our premise is that its best chances for survival lie with those who, like us, have come to appreciate its extraordinary beauty.

Preface to the 1990 Edition

Since the first edition of this book was published in 1976, there have been many changes, some good, some not so. With the Wilderness Bill of 1984, 65,000 new acres were added to the Mokelumne Wilderness, nearly tripling the existing acreage. The most significant addition for backpackers is a parcel that includes Beebe Lake, formerly plundered by jeepsters. Unfortunately, Squaw Ridge and Lost Lake remain open to motorized vehicles.

As we predicted, the area has also increased in popularity. It is still wonderful, beautiful, and mostly wild, but if you are venturing into the Wilderness Area on a weekend, you would be well advised to apply for your permit in advance. And, needless to say, there is increased need to be thoughtful for the interests of others.

Round Top Peak

Table of Contents

Introduction

THE HIGH SIERRA HIK-ING GUIDES by the editors of Wilderness Press are the first *complete* guides to the famous High Sierra. Each guide covers at least one 15-minute U.S.G.S. topographic quadrangle, which is an area about 14 miles east-west by 17 miles north-south. The first page shows the location of the area covered by this guide.

There is a great and increasing demand for literature about America's favorite wilderness, John Muir's "Range of Light." To meet this demand, we have undertaken this guide series. The purpose of each book in the series is threefold: first, to provide a reliable basis for planning a trip; second, to serve as a field guide while you are on the trail; and third, to stimulate you to further field investigation and background reading. In each guide, there is a minimum of 100 described miles of trails, and the descriptions are supplemented with maps and other logistical and background information. HIGH SIERRA HIK-ING GUIDES are based on first-hand observation. There is absolutely no substitute for walking the trails, so we walked all the trails.

In planning this series, we chose the 15-minute quadrangle as the unit because—though every way of dividing the Sierra is arbitrary—the topographic quadrangle map ("topo map") is the chosen aid of almost every wilderness traveler. In addition to the *Silver Lake* quadrangle, this book covers the hiking trails in the western part of the *Markleeville* quadrangle, which adjoins *Silver Lake* on the east. Inside the back cover of this book is a large map of all the area the book covers, showing described trails and cross-country routes. With this map, you can always get where you want to go, with a minimum of detours or wasted effort.

One other thing the wilderness traveler will need: a wilderness permit from the Forest Service. A permit is required for an overnight stay or even a day visit to the Mokelumne Wilderness. You can obtain your permit by mail or in person at the ranger stations listed below, except that those with no listed address require a personal visit.

El Dorado National Forest, Amador District

Amador Ranger District Office, 1 mile east of Buckhorn just off Highway 88 on Silver Drive. Address: Star Route 3, Pioneer, CA 95666. Tel. (209) 295-4251.

In summer, the Forest Service maintains a visitor information booth at Carson Pass.

Stanislaus National Forest, Calaveras District

Arnold Ranger Station, Arnold CA 95223. Tel. (209) 795-1381.

There's also a ranger station 2½ miles west of Lake Alpine on Highway 4.

Toiyabe National Forest, Alpine Ranger District

Markleeville Ranger Station, Markleeville CA 96120. Tel. (916) 495-2182.

The History

SUMMERING IN THE CARson Pass area has been going on a long time—several thousand years in fact. The Washoe Indians, winter residents of the Great Basin east of the Sierra, spent the summer months high in the mountains fishing, hunting, and trading with tribes of the western foothills. Lake Tahoe was the center of their summer activity but they frequented the *Silver Lake* area as well; and traces of their occupancy—potholes, pounding stones and an occasional arrowhead—can still be found on the granite ridges of the countryside. Some existing trails were once their trading routes.

The Washoe were a simple people with little in the way of technology. Their baskets, however, woven of willow and colored red and black with rosebud and fern root, were works of art and, until quite recently, a source of income from tourists. Like most primitive peoples, they identified with nature and developed a rich mythology to explain its mysteries. The mountain lakes, for example, were said to be the remnants of a great flood caused by a powerful creature called the Water Baby, in retaliation for its captivity by a mischievous weasel. A modern version of the same myth attributes the San Francisco earthquake of 1906 to the angry work of a Water Baby that was captured accidentally by a San Francisco fisherman and subsequently incarcerated in the city's aquarium. Moral: beware of attempting to harness the primitive forces of nature.

What happened to the Washoe with the coming of the white settler is a familiar and depressing story, neatly implied in the Washoe word for the newcomers, "mushege," meaning both a fierce animal and a bad-tempered man. A small tribe (probably no more than 600 in number by the 19th century) and generally peaceful, they quickly became dependent on the white man's culture and economy. Suffering both dislocation and poverty, they turned inward from their problems to embrace the peyote cult as part of their religion.

Another Indian tribe, the Miwok, occasionally ranged from the west as far as the upper Mokelumne, but they apparently tended to stick to the foothills. It was they, however, who gave the name to the river: "Mokel-um-i" means "people of Mokel," Mokel being a Miwok village situated near what is now Stockton. According to the anthropologist Alfred Kroeber, however, "Moquelumnan is an artificially derived synonym for Miwok."

Among the first white men encountered by the Washoe were the members of a famous expedition led by John C. Fremont, with Kit Carson as his guide. In the winter of 1844 the party, having come south from Oregon east of the Sierra, made their way to what is now Grovers Hot Springs, a few miles west of Markleeville. The Washoe befriended them, and warned them not to try to cross the mountains in the winter— "rock upon rock . . . snow upon snow," one Indian guide conveyed in sign language—but the "mushege" paid no heed. Forcing their way west to Charity Valley and then north to Faith Valley, they established a camp from which Fremont and Carson climbed Elephants Back, just south of Carson Pass. Fremont's diary describes what they saw.

> Far below us, dimmed by the distance, was a large, snowless valley, bounded on the western side by a low range of mountains which Carson recognized with delight as the mountains bordering the coast. "There," he said, "is the little mountain—it is fifteen years since I saw it; but I am just as sure as if I had seen it yesterday."

The "little mountain" was Mt. Diablo, and from the sighting Fremont and Carson were able to chart their route to Sutter's Fort, their destination.

Continuing to scout the region, Fremont climbed a peak north of Carson Pass "from which we had a beautiful view of a mountain lake at our feet, about fifteen miles in length and so entirely surrounded by mountains that we could not discover an outlet." The lake Fremont saw that wintry day came to be known as Tahoe, and his climb, of what was probably

Red Lake Peak, is described by the late Sierra historian Francis Farquhar as the "first identifiable mountain ascent in the Sierra."

The cold and the physical exertion took its toll as the Indians warned it would—two of the men were driven insane and one wandered off, never to be seen again—but gradually the party made its way over the mountain heights and then proceeded down the South Fork of the American River to Sutter's Fort. Whether they actually crossed at Carson Pass or at some unidentified pass to the south is a matter of dispute among the historians, but the inscription "Kit Carson-1844" was found carved on a tree near Carson Pass, and that is enough for us True Believers.

Four years later, in 1848, the Mormon Battalion chose the Carson Pass route for their return to the Great Salt Lake from their battles in the Spanish-American War. It was they who gave its name to Tragedy Spring—the location at which three of their number were massacred, apparently by Indians—and to Hope Valley. And it was they who widened the route over Carson Pass, previously only a trail, into a wagon road that soon became one of the major emigrant routes across the Sierra—the Carson Emigrant route. On the east side of the pass, the route was practically congruent with what is now Highway 88, up Carson (Woodfords) Canyon and through Hope Valley to Red Lake. In the 1850s this part of the route became a toll road, and a stage station at Hope Valley was operated by J. L. Stevens, after whom Stevens Peak was named. From the western end of Red Lake the road climbed steeply up to the pass on a route so precipitous it was known as "Devil's Ladder." Portions of the road and grooves on old trees, used as anchors in pulling wagons and equipment up by rope, are still discernible.

From Carson Pass the road descended to what is now Caples Lake, named after James "Doc" Caples who in 1849 saw the lake on his way west, and later came back to settle. Then known as "Summit Lake," later as "Clear Lake," and still later as "Twin Lakes," this feature was actually two lakes surrounded by meadow. Years later, when the lower lake was dammed by PG&E, the basin filled with water to form a single reservoir.

The present road from Caples Lake over the Carson Spur was not constructed until later in the last century. The emigrant route crossed between the two twin lakes and ascended south past Emigrant Lake to what is sometimes called Emigrant Pass but which the emigrant called, West Pass, and which in this book we will call, West Pass. West Pass, at an elevation of 9560 feet, is claimed to be the highest point to have been reached by stage coaches in the United States. From there, the road followed Squaw Ridge southward to Plasse Trading Post, then veered west, descending to Mud Lake and meeting what is now Highway 88 near Allen Ranch. The entire emigrant route has been marked by signs and is easily followed.

Paralleling the Carson-Emigrant road to the south was a trans-Sierra Indian trail occasionally used by prospectors. In 1850 John A. Ebbetts, leading a group of prospectors and engineers over the pass and finding little snow, recommended it as a route for a railroad crossing. His recommendation was never accepted, but efforts were made to get the State Legislature to construct a wagon road across the pass. In 1856 a group of businessmen, tired of waiting for the legislature, raised money to build their own road. Known as the "Big Trees-Carson Valley Road," it paralleled the present Ebbetts Pass highway between the Calaveras Big Trees and Hermit Valley, then turned north to Blue Lakes, Border Ruffian Pass (where, legend has it, Joaquin Murieta and his "gang of bandits" exacted their own form of tolls) and on to Hope Valley, where it joined the Carson Pass emigrant route. Portions of the old road (from Lake Alpine to Bear Valley) have been cleared as a hiking trail by volunteer groups.

The Big Trees-Carson Valley Road served as a main emigrant

route for two years until 1858, when a good road became available over Luther Pass and Echo Summit. The latter route was part of one of the most bizarre experiments in the history of the west: the transportation of Bactrian camels (yes, camels) to Nevada, where they were used for a brief period to carry salt from the Lahontan Basin to the mills of Virginia City. The camels terrified the horses, however, and the Nevada legislature adopted a law prohibiting camels from traveling on highways or entering towns after dark.

Finally, in the early 1860s, a toll road, then called the Big Trees and Carson Valley Turnpike, and now called the Ebbetts Pass road or Highway 4, was constructed from Hermit Valley over the summit to Markleeville, and the old emigrant routes fell into disuse.

The construction of the Ebbetts Pass road coincided with an event of momentous importance for the area—the discovery of silver by a group of Scandinavian miners at Silver Mountain, just east of the crest on the headwaters of the Carson River near Ebbetts Pass. By 1863 thousands of prospectors were pouring into the tiny community first known as Köngsberg and later as Silver Mountain City.

Prospecting extended from Silver Mountain to the surrounding area. A mining district called Raymond, after a U.S. Mineral Examiner, embraced the upper portion of Pleasant Valley Creek Canyon and included a small mining hamlet called Raymond City in a canyon north of what is now Raymond Peak. Another district, called Alpine, included Markleeville (settled by Jacob Marklee in 1861) and the lower portions of Pleasant Valley and Indian Creek Canyon. As far away as Summit City Canyon, in what became the Mokelumne district, two small towns, Upper and Lower Summit City, came into existence.

Mining culture developed various forms of amusement in addition to the usual saloons and houses of prostitution. Each year a fair was held in Hope Valley, and a track was constructed for horseracing. In the winter, ski-jumping contests were held, the first and most famous sponsored by "Snowshoe" Thompson, who carried the U.S. mail in winter over routes impassable by horse or wagon. It was a lively time.

But the prosperity and excitement were brief. By 1868 the Silver Mountain district began to be depleted, and interest shifted eastward, to the Monitor district. In 1873 the U.S. Government demonetized silver, putting an end to mining in the entire area. The once-bustling mining towns quickly became ghost towns. Connecting roads fell into disuse and deteriorated. True, resorts continued to be operated along the Carson Pass Road, especially at Silver Lake and Caples Lake, and cattle and dairy ranches which had developed in the meadowlands continued. But otherwise, the countryside returned almost to the wilderness condition in which Fremont and Carson had found it a generation earlier.

Except for the construction by PG&E of control dams at four major lakes feeding into the Mokelumne River, and the reservoirs at Bear River and Salt Springs, the physical character of the area between the two highways has changed little over the last 100 years. The portion east of the Sierra crest was proclaimed a national forest in 1908, and the portion west of the crest in 1910. In 1964, 50,400 acres on the western slope within the Eldorado and Stanislaus national forests were established as the Mokelumne Wilderness, closed to vehicular traffic. The Forest Service has recently acquired an additional 600 acres of private land in the Ladeux Meadow area, which it proposes to add to the wilderness area. As in many areas, the Forest Service has been under constant political pressure from lumber interests to allow more cutting, and on occasion it has yielded, to the detriment of trails and the adjacent countryside. It is also under pressure from jeepsters who want to continue using the old emigrant and miners' roads as obstacle courses, but it attempts to offer other routes at lower elevations instead. It can use your political assistance.

The Geology

THE EBBETTS PASS-Carson Pass region lies on the crest of the Sierra Nevada, a great fault block of the earth's crust, which about 5 or 10 million years ago was uplifted about 6000 feet on its east side and tilted to a slope of 80 feet per mile as you descend westward. In the Owens Valley region the Sierra Nevada is bounded on the east by a single large fault scarp—as is so dramatically evident to the visitor there—but in our region the eastern boundary of the range is far more complex. The drop from the Sierra crest to the desert valleys on the east is accomplished in stages along several faults, which trend nearly north-south, and each fault dies out at its south end as it approaches the Sierra crest. In the latitude of Ebbetts and Carson passes, the easternmost of the three major faults runs along the west side of Antelope and Slinkard valleys and dies out somewhere near Leavitt Meadow on the Sonora Pass road. The second fault runs along the west side of Carson Valley, and enters the mountains near Woodfords. It forms the east front of Hawkins Peak, passes through Grovers Hot Springs and Pleasant Valley, and eventually dies out in Nobel Canyon north of Tryon Peak. A branch of this fault passes along the west side of Hope Valley and dies out near Blue Lakes. The westernmost fault runs along the west side of Lake Tahoe, and dies out southward in the upper Truckee Valley near Echo Summit.

Between the faults are blocks of the earth's crust each of which is generally higher on the east and tilted down on the west. The crests of these blocks stand at about the same elevation, on the average. The stream drainage pattern in this area is determined by this fault pattern—the streams flow north, down valleys they are cutting along the fault zones. West of the Sierra crest, the streams generally flow southwest, following the *fall line*—a line that goes directly downslope.

The rocks of the Sierra are much older than the mountains. In age and origin they can be conveniently divided into three groups.

Metamorphic rocks. The oldest are the metamorphic rocks, which were once sand, shale, limy mud and lava flows on the sea floor. Later they were altered by great heat and pressure into slate, schist, quartzite, marble and greenstone, as well as a variety of more unusual metamorphic rocks. The heat and pressure that changed the rocks was due to their deep burial under rocks formed later, and also due to contact with the hot *magma* that formed the granitic rocks described below. Very few patches of metamorphic rock remain in the Ebbetts Pass-Carson Pass area. The largest are 1) some patches on the east slope of Red Lake and Stevens peaks, north of Carson Pass; 2) a body of schist and slate in the low hills between Red Lake and Hope and Faith valleys; 3) a northwest-trending belt 3 miles long and ½ mile wide on the southwest slope of Hawkins Peak; and 4) a complex patch of metamorphic rocks about 1½ miles east of Lake Alpine on Highway 4.

Granitic rocks. Next in age are the granitic rocks. Between 120 and 80 million years ago, large bodies of granitic magma invaded the Sierra's metamorphic rocks from below, and upon cooling eventually crystallized to become coarse-grained mainly light-colored rocks, which form the basement of the Sierra Nevada. These rocks consist mainly of interlocking crystalline grains of the minerals quartz and feldspar, with lesser amounts of the minerals biotite (black mica) and hornblende (a dark-green to black mineral that looks like little bits of very hard charcoal embedded in the rock). The commonest of the granitic rocks are granodiorite, a light gray rock with abundant crystals of hornblende and biotite scattered through it, and quartz monzonite, a faintly pink rock, lacking hornblende crystals but containing biotite and commonly characterized by large, rectangular crystals of feldspar, as much as 2 inches on a side and scattered through the finer crystalline rock.

The granitic rock crystallized and cooled under a cover several thousand feet thick, which later was stripped away by erosion, many tens of millions of years ago. You will notice that this granitic rock is broken by *joints* (parallel, nearly plane fractures) spaced a few feet to a few tens of feet apart. Erosion tends to proceed fastest along these joints.

Volcanic rocks. The youngest rocks in this part of the Sierra are mainly volcanic rocks that were erupted between 20 and 7 million years ago. They flowed over the surface of the granitic rocks after the latter had been eroded down to about their present levels. The vents from which these volcanic flows erupted later became plugged with cooled, congealed lava, which filled the volcanoes' necks. Later the surrounding rock was eroded away, while these neck fillings—being composed of harder rocks—persisted to become the highest peaks of the

lava on Horse Canyon trail

region: Hawkins Peak, Elephants Back, Silver Peak, Highland Peak, Lookout Peak and Round Top.

The earliest of the volcanic eruptions were apparently white rhyolitic ash flows, which were mostly eroded away after they were erupted, and are now preserved as only a few patches. The great bulk of the volcanic rocks consists of andesite, a dark-brown to gray rock, which was erupted mainly as breccias (accumulations of angular fragments) which in some way were quickly saturated with water, and which flowed down the west slope of the Sierra as hot mudflows. Eruptions from any particular vent may have occurred once every hundred thousand years or so, and between them, running water eroded the mudflows and their interbedded conglomerates are in the Carson Spur between Silver Lake and Kirkwood Meadow. The volcanic rocks once entirely covered this part of the Sierra, but they have been largely stripped away from the crest and the west side of the range. They are preserved here as remnants along the drainage divides.

The prevolcanic drainage was obliterated by the floods of lava, and the present drainage pattern of the west slope of the Sierra evolved during the accumulation of the volcanic rocks, as the successive lavas flowed down and filled each new river channel that erosion had created. The rivers we now see on the western slope are essentially those that existed at the end of the period of volcanic activity, about 6 or 7 million years ago. Mainly, the effect of erosion has been to cut a series of deep canyons on the west slope (American River, Mokelumne River, Stanislaus River) and between them to strip away much of the volcanic deposits and the weathered granitic rocks beneath them.

Many times during the last 3 million years the highest parts of the Sierra have been partly buried by glaciers, and the present topography of the highland area is the product of glaciation. Only the glaciers of the last hundred thousand years have left clear marks on the landscape: in the form of bowl-shaped cirques at the heads of canyons; in the U-shaped cross sections of some of the canyons and valleys; in the abundance of rock-basin lakes, in the glacially smoothed, scratched and polished knobs that dot the plateau areas; in the poorly sorted deposits of boulders, sand and clay (collectively called *till*) which are heaped up into irregular ridges called *moraines;* and in the scattered giant boulders, clearly far from their place of origin, that we call glacial *erratics.*

In the Mokelumne area, ice of the last glaciations accumulated in cirques as low as 7700 feet on the north side of the Carson Pass road west of Tragedy Spring, but most of the areas of ice accumulation (where snow persisted from winter to winter) were above 8000 feet. The Sierra crest and the slopes west of it received most of the snow; hence, the mountains east of the crest had smaller glaciers or none at all, even though they were more than 9000 feet high.

Most of the upland between Ebbetts Pass and Carson Pass was covered with ice. Ice flowed down the Silver Fork of the American, and its tributaries Caples and North Tragedy creeks, roughly to their junction. It flowed down the Bear River to Lower Bear River Reservoir, and down the Mokelumne an unknown distance below Salt Springs Valley Reservoir. It probably flowed down the Stanislaus (North Fork) about as far as Ramsey, at 4800 feet altitude. During the Ice Age, glaciers advanced and retreated about 50 times or more. The last major glaciation ended just over 10,000 years ago. We have to conclude that if past cycles repeat themselves, we will enter another continental-scale ice age in about 1000 years!

Campgrounds and Resorts

For those nights between day trips, and for that night of acclimation when you first arrive in the mountains from the lowlands (to avoid "elevation sickness" it is always best to spend a night in the higher elevation before you start hiking) there are a variety of car-camping possibilities and, for comfort-seekers, a few resort accommodations. All of the car camping is at U.S. Forest Service campsites. All have tables, fireplaces, toilets and running water except as otherwise indicated. Almost all charge a small fee.

A. Silver Lake Area

1. *Car Camping*

Silver Lake East. Just north of Silver Lake, off Highway 88. 59 campsites, trailers. Some campsites with view of the lake.

Silver Lake West. On the opposite side of Highway 88 from Silver Lake East. 38 campsites, trailers.

Martin Meadows Overflow. Three miles east of Silver Lake on Highway 88, used when the Silver Lake campgrounds are full. Chemical toilets only.

2. *Resorts*

Kit Carson Lodge. ½ mile off Highway 88 from the north end of the spillway at Silver Lake. (Signed *Kit Carson.*) Cabins, a few motel units, restaurant, store, beach, boat rentals. Rustically luxurious.

Kaye's Resort. At the north end of Silver Lake, near the south end of the spillway. Store, restaurant, boat rentals and cabins overlooking the lake. Open year-round.

Plasse's Resort. At the south end of Silver Lake. Store, horses, trailer park, some cabin facilities. Operated by the family of one of the earliest settlers.

B. Carson Pass-Caples Lake Area

1. *Car Camping*

Caples Lake. Across the highway from Caples Lake Resort at Caples Lake. 35 campsites, trailers.

Woods Lake. 2 miles south of Highway 88 between Caples Lake and Carson Pass. The road to the lake is in the form of a "Y," the top two branches leading from Highway 88 at distances of 2½ and 3¾ miles, respectively, east of Caples Lake Resort. 19 campsites, no trailers. Heavily used.

2. *Resorts*

Caples Lake Resort. At Caples Lake. Store, boat rentals, coffee shop, rooms, gas, phone and cabins with lake view. Open year-round.

Sorenson's. In Hope Valley on Highway 88, ½ mile east of Highway 89 junction. Cabins, store, restaurant, guided tours of Emigrant Trail. Open year-round.

C. Highway 4

1. *Car Camping*

Big Meadow. 8½ miles west of Lake Alpine on Highway 4; 69 campsites, trailers.

Sand Flat. 8½ miles west of Lake Alpine on Highway 4 then 2 miles south on a steep, unimproved Forest Service road (7N12), 6 campsites.

Silver Tip. On Highway 4, 1 mile west of Lake Alpine. 24 campsites, trailers.

Lake Alpine. On the north shore of Lake Alpine off Highway 4 across from Lake Alpine Lodge. 28 campsites, trailers.

Pine Marten. ¼ mile southeast of the east end of Lake Alpine. 23 campsites, trailers. (There are some campsites set aside for backpackers on the road in.)

Silver Valley. Just beyond Pine Marten, on the same Forest Service road. 26 campsites, trailers.

Mosquito Lakes. On Highway 4, 6 miles east of Lake Alpine. Day use only.

Pacific Valley. On Highway 4, 8 miles east of Lake Alpine. 5 official campsites, but holds hundreds; trailers.

2. *Resorts*

Lake Alpine Resort. At Lake Alpine. Cabins, restaurant, store, gas, phone.

Bear Valley. Just north of Highway 4, 3 miles west of Lake Alpine. Lodge, condominiums, restaurant, gas, phone.

D. Lower Bear River-Salt Springs Area

1. *Car Camping*

Lumberyard. On Highway 88, 20 miles east of Pioneer, across the road from what was the ranger station. Unpleasant but bearable for one night.

Lower Bear River. From the signed junction 2 miles east of Lumberyard on Highway 88, a paved Forest Service road descends 3 miles to Lower Bear River Reservoir. These campsites are on the north side, adjacent to the Bear River Resort. 10 campsites, trailers.

South Shore. On the south shore of Lower Bear River Reservoir. 20 campsites, small trailers only. Pleasant. Fee $2.00.

Mokelumne. From what was the Lumberyard Ranger Station on Highway 88, 20 miles east of Pioneer, Ellis Road (signed) winds down for about 12 miles to Salt Springs Reservoir. Eight miles down, it comes to this campground along the river. 12 campsites, no trailers. Purify river water before using.

White Azalea. 1½ miles past Mokelumne Campground on the way to Salt Springs Reservoir. 6 campsites, no trailers. Purify river water before using.

2. *Resorts*

Bear River Resort. On the north shore of Lower Bear River Reservoir. Cabins, store, restaurant, gas, phone.

The Trails

WITHIN THE AREA COVERED by this book are several levels of trails. At one extreme are what the Forest Service calls "Level 3" trails, graded and maintained for horse travel. Most of these are in the immediate vicinity of Silver Lake. At the other extreme are "Level 1" trails, or "trailways," which have been marked with ribbons and/or blazes, and are partly cleared of brush from time to time, but which, with admirable restraint, the Forest Service leaves in a fairly primitive condition for the adventurous hiker. In between is the largest category—the "Level 2" trails—which are maintained for hikers but which, because of terrain or trail condition, are not particularly suitable for equestrians.

In addition to these designated trails, we have mapped and described a number of cross-country routes which are within the ability of the average hiker in good physical condition who has had some experience with cross-country travel and is equipped with a map and compass. We also include in the "cross-country" category those trails that are so poorly marked or so seldom traveled in whole or in part as to impose requirements similar to those just mentioned.

In 1979 the U.S. Geological Survey published larger, 7½-minute maps of parts of the area covered by this book. These include the *Bear River Reservoir* and *Mokelumne Peak* quadrangles, covering the southwest and southeast parts, respectively, of the *Silver Lake* 15-minute quadrangle; and the *Carson Pass* and *Pacific Valley* quadrangles, covering the northwest and southwest parts, respectively, of the *Markleeville* 15-minute quadrangle. These are good maps to have along, but for trip planning and general route following, the 15-minute quadrangle in this book is still the easiest to use. Even the new 7½-minute maps do not accurately show some of the trails. Our main objective in this book has been to map and describe the trails and cross-country routes in such a way that the reader will not get lost.

A second objective has been to provide the reader with sufficient information to enable him to plan a trip that will suit his tastes, time and capabilities. In that connection, we make suggestions for day and backpack trips of various lengths, but in such a manner that you can discover the country in your own way, planning your own routes and stopping places, on the basis of the information provided.

To facilitate trip planning, we have grouped the trail and route descriptions according to starting areas: Silver Lake; the Caples Lake-Carson Pass area; the Ebbetts Pass Road; and Lower Bear River Reservoir. To some extent the assignment of trails to a particular area is arbitrary; for example, we describe the trip down the Mokelumne River in Section 3 (trips from the Ebbetts Pass Road), though the trip can be made from several other starting points as well. For such situations we provide appropriate cross references in the text.

Within each geographical area we also group the trails into "day trips" and "backpack trips" and that, too, is somewhat arbitrary. In general, we have limited day trips to 12 miles. Some of the day trips can be made as backpack trips, and vice versa. We leave that to your discretion and tastes.

We also have a third objective in this chapter—to call your attention to considerations of wilderness preservation relating to actions the government might take and things you should be careful about in the way you use the backcountry. Wherever you backpack, you will need a fire permit from the Forest Service, and if you enter the wilderness area you will need a wilderness permit as well. Both are available free at any ranger station. A list of ranger stations appears in the Introduction. In addition, we urge that you follow these basic rules:

1. **Avoid pollution by burying human waste at least 6–8 inches deep.**
2. **Use a stove rather than firewood.**
3. **Use only biodegradable soaps.**

4. Do not wash in or close to streams or lakes.
5. Carry out all garbage—certainly your own, and if possible that which you find left by others.
6. Avoid camping in heavily populated areas.

One further work of caution: Much of this area is canyon country, and that means rattlesnakes. You can walk for weeks—as we did—and not see one; but they are there, particularly in the lower elevations. The Forest Service reports no incidents of people being bitten, but they do report snake bites of horses and dogs. If you are planning a trip down Summit City Canyon, or one of the other tributary canyons of the Mokelumne River, we recommend leaving your dog at home. If you are walking through thick underbrush or climbing rocks in a canyon, be careful where you put your feet and your hands. And carry a rattlesnake kit. Subject to those precautions, enjoy yourself; you're still safer than on the streets.

Section 1   Trips from Silver Lake

> Silver Lake is one of the most beautiful sheets of water in the world, and a sojourn on its banks in the Summer is one of the most pleasantest enjoyments possible. . . .
>
> Mason, *History of Amador County* (1881)

The historian's comments, while somewhat ungrammatically expressed, reflect the enthusiasm with which people regarded Silver Lake a century ago when its shores accommodated one of the finest hotels to be found in the area. He tells us of "a delicate, feeble woman, who had to be lifted into a carriage at the beginning of the journey," but who improved so rapidly in a few weeks' stay "as to get up in the morning and, from very exuberance of feeling, give a half dozen Indian yells that could be heard a mile, or catch up a pair of oars and row a half-mile out into the lake, singing and shouting in a way that would bring the police down on her or cause an examination for lunacy if done in a city."

My family's enthusiasm for Silver Lake is no less unbounded. For years we have been spending part of our summers there, camping out or staying at Kit Carson Lodge, enjoying the magnificence of the scenery—the tree-fringed lake, encompassed by white granite ridges and dark volcanic ridges, with the strange, inspiring obelisk of Thunder Peak towering above, brilliantly red in the sunset. But as magnificent as the lake itself is, even more so is the surrounding countryside, and it is that we would like to share with you.

DAY HIKES

Sec. 1.1   Granite Lake and Hidden Lake (1–3 miles one way)

These two lakes, both of them less than an hour's walk from Silver Lake, are ideal picnic-fishing locations for the non-energetic hiker. A variety of trails in this area, some unsigned but nevertheless easily located, afford opportunity for more vigorous and diversified walking. Because of their easy accessibility and consequent liability to overuse, camping on them during the summer months is not recommended.

The short route to Granite Lake (just under one mile) begins a few yards below a parking area on the road to what used to be called Camp Minkalo, on the east side of Silver Lake. The first part of the trail was built by Campfire Girls as a bypass of the older trail, which took hikers through the middle of their camp. The objective is admirable, the execution whimsical. In relaxed disregard of the contour lines, the trail winds over granite ledges to the southeast, then veers south along another granite ledge and crosses Squaw Creek on a wooden bridge. Just across the bridge is an attractive picnic spot, complete with a sandy beach and a small waterfall. A few yards beyond is a signed junction. The trail to the right continues to climb for about ¼ mile, then drops to the level of Silver Lake, which meets an older lakeside trail, which follows the lake front south to Plasse's resort 1½ miles from the junction.

Taking the left branch at the junction, we walk through a lightly wooded area which affords views of Thimble Peak in the northeast. Then the trail climbs steeply over granite lined with manzanita, offering increasingly open views of Silver Lake and the Crystal Range to the north, and soon arrives at the outlet stream from Granite Lake. From there it is but 200 yards to the lake itself—situated in a granite basin that has fine slabs for sunning and a small island near the west shore that makes a nice goal for swimmers. The surrounding forest is mainly red fir and lodgepole pine, with a few mountain hemlocks and an occasional Jeffrey pine on the adjacent ridges. Small level areas on the southwest and northeast sides provide poor-to-fair camping.

When you are ready to leave, you may of course retrace your steps, but if, like me, you find that prospect uninspiring, you have the following alternatives.

First, you may walk from *Granite Lake to Plasse* (1¾ miles) by taking the trail toward Hidden Lake which starts from the southeast corner of Granite Lake. The first ½ mile or so proceeds on sandy duff through a heavily forested, nearly level area past a series of volcanic rock masses. Another ¼ mile through a flat, meadowy area brings you to a pond on the west side of which is a trail sign that points ahead toward Hidden Lake and back toward Granite Lake. Just behind the sign, heading to the west, is a well-blazed but unsigned trail, which is the one you want. Dropping somewhat steeply to the west and south, in ¾ mile the trail becomes a logging road, and in another ¼ mile, after crossing two streams, it arrives at Plasse's resort. The trail is easier to locate coming from the east than coming from Plasse, so at least the first time it is best to take it downhill. From Plasse, you may walk back to your car via the lakeside trail mentioned above.

Alternatively, you may walk from *Granite Lake to Hidden Lake* (just under 2 miles) and then to Plasse (another mile). The first part of that trail, to the sign by the pond, is described in the preceding paragraph. From there the Hidden Lake Trail climbs moderately up and over a small ridge (at the bottom of which is an old side trail to the west, connecting with the Plasse trail) and then begins to curve east, arriving in ½ mile at the outlet from Hidden Lake. The trail follows the north side of the outlet for several hundred yards, then fords it and climbs steeply, arriving at Hidden Lake in another ¼ mile. Hidden Lake is a bit cool for swimming but good campsites are found on the west side.

From *Hidden Lake to Plasse* there are two routes, the shorter of which (1 mile) is unsigned and not much used, but well blazed and easily followed. Starting about 100 yards west of the lake, it leaves the main trail and contours west for ¼ mile with only a slight drop in altitude. It then drops moderately steeply to the northwest to meet the Hidden Lake outlet stream and descends alongside the stream through a granitic area with cascading creeklets and colorful tiny meadows. Then the trail contours west, away from the stream, descends gently to the northwest, fords a stream and arrives at the trailhead for the Squaw Ridge Trail (see the next paragraph).

The longer route from Hidden Lake to Plasse (just over 2 miles) starts from the west shore of Hidden Lake, where a sign reads *Granite Lake 2* (north) and *Plasse 3* (south). Proceeding southwest, the trail crosses a stream, rounds a meadow and climbs steeply south, skirting the north edge of a beautiful meadow at the base of a ridge. Then it arrives at a signed junction with the Squaw Ridge Trail (Sec. 1.6). A few yards north of the junction is an outlook affording spectacular views of Silver Lake and the Desolation Valley peaks to the north as well as of the Thunder Peak-Thimble Peak ridge. Turning right (north) on the Squaw Ridge Trail we drop on switchbacks down the face of the ridge, cross a stream and stroll gradually downhill through verdant meadows full of lupine, mule ears and forget-me-nots. The last ½ mile drops steeply at first through a densely wooded area, then levels off to the trailhead, located 200 yards east of the Stockton Municipal Camp and about 300 yards south of Plasse. At the trailhead is a barely legible sign reading *Wilderness Area 6 miles ahead—Permit Required.* To the right (east) of the trail sign and across the stream is the trail to Hidden Lake described in the preceding paragraph.

Thunder Peak

Sec. 1.2   Horse Canyon Trail to Squaw Ridge (5½ miles)

The canyon from which this trail derives its name swoops down the east slope of Squaw Ridge to Summit City Creek at a pitch such that few but superathletes or unrequited masochists would regard it as part of a day's outing from Silver Lake. The portion of the trail from Silver Lake to Squaw Ridge, however, is a staple part of any Silver Lake hiking diet. As access for exploring the side country, as a segment in a longer loop trip, or simply as a way of getting up in the world and enjoying some great scenery for a day, the trail is a rare treat.

In bygone days the trail began at a summer-home tract on the northeast side of Silver Lake and passed through a Boy Scout camp (El Dorado) on its way. To avoid disturbing cabin owners and Scouts, the Forest Service recently constructed a new initial section of the trail which, though longer, provides an easier grade and in some ways a more scenic route.

Beginning at a signed trailhead at a tiny parking area on the east side of Highway 88, just 0.8 mile north of Silver Lake, the trail climbs gradually through a pleasantly cool red-fir forest at the base of the reddish cliffs of Thunder Peak, winding its way among huge, gray pieces of lava which, through weathering, have taken on some grotesque and wonderful shapes. After a long mile the trail begins to climb steadily, and passes two unsigned junctions with older trails from the cabin areas and Camp El Dorado before arriving, 2½ miles out, at a runoff stream not shown on the map which, in a normal mid-summer, provides the first available water on the hike.

From this stream the trail continues to traverse, first over open slopes dotted with red firs and luxuriant in mule ears, providing fine views of the surrounding ridges. Then it leads through a heavy forest once more, the floor strewn with pieces of brittle red fir broken off by winter storms. Leaving this forest we stroll onto open, rocky slopes with many large granite boulders and tiny meadows containing numerous wildflowers, including lupine, yarrow milfoil, collinsia, phlox, paintbrush, daisy, groundsel and forget-me-nots. In ½ mile from the first stream our trail reaches a second, more substantial stream which tumbles down from the meadow lying below the ridge that connects Thunder and Thimble peaks. Even if you are not making a climb of the peaks, a side trip up and around this meadowy bowl is worth the effort. Fed by melting snows well into summer, the bowl is a sheer delight, full of mule ears and other flowers and affording marvelous views of the countryside.

The trail crosses this stream and continues rather steeply up its east bank, enabling us to enjoy its sunlit chutes and cascades. Then the trail veers east and climbs steeply to the crest of a granite ridge, arriving at a natural lookout point presided over by a solitary juniper. From here you can see Silver Lake, Thunder Peak, and the top of Thimble Peak. The trail levels off for a bit, dips to cross a flower-flanked third stream and climbs back up to Thimble Peak's southwest spur. From here you have even more panoramic views of the Thunder-Thimble-Emigrant peaks ridge system and of the inclined meadowy bowls that lie just below this ridge. The trail contours around Thimble Peak through these meadows, filled with flowers nourished by the rich lava soil and watered by late-melting snows. Purple lupine, yellow mule ears and buttercups, and brilliant red paintbrush mingle their colors and textures with sagebrush, columbine, collinsia, cinquefoil, wallflower, corn lily, woolly sunflower, sulfur flower and pennyroyal in one of the most lavish flower displays in *Silver Lake*.

From the southwest spur of Thimble Peak our route continues east, contouring north of a large, meadowy bowl, which often has snow into mid-July, making the trail sometimes difficult to follow. Soon the top of Thimble Peak, with a recently built chair-lift tower on its north slope, becomes visible. The trail then heads southeast, climbing at a moderate grade through subalpine meadows laced with runoff streams and flowered with whorled penstemon, pussypaws and sagebrush, to arrive at a sign reading ½ *Scout Carson Lake* (Sec. 1.3). A half mile beyond is the top of Squaw Ridge and a signed junction with the Squaw Ridge Jeep Trail.

The jeep trail is a portion of the old Carson emigrant route. A left turn (north) brings you in ½ mile to what we will call West Pass. Listen to an emigrant's voice from 1855:

> As we approached the pass the scenery became more grand and imposing. The ridge which the road follows is very narrow and falls away precipitately on either side into deep canyons; those forming the heads of the North Fork of the Mokelumne are of white granite and apparently totally impassable.

Sec. 1.3   Side Trip to Scout Carson, Summit Meadow and Devil's Hole Lake (cross-country, ½–6 miles)

These three lakes, below and west of Squaw Ridge, are accessible only by cross-country travel. All three have fishing and swimming and good campsites, and they provide a pleasant excursion off the main Horse Canyon Trail.

Scout Carson Lake is the most accessible, situated just over ¼ mile from the Horse Canyon Trail (Sec. 1.2) on a signed route. Heading south from the sign, the route goes almost level across partly marshy country to the lake. The lake is shallow, and camping at the inlet on the hemlock-clothed north side is fair.

The route from Scout Carson to Summit Meadow Lake (1½ miles) is a bit more difficult. Heading south-to-southwest, follow the stream which runs closest to the ridge. Just before reaching the lake, the stream drops sharply over falls, then bubbles through a meadow. Fair-to-good camp spots are on the east side and on the plateau above the lake to the north.

From Summit Meadow to Devils Hole Lake (1 mile) the unmarked route proceeds southwest up to a rocky saddle and down the other side. The lake can also be reached by a steep trail from the Squaw Ridge Jeep Trail at Martell Flats.

Scout Carson Lake

Sec. 1.4 Martin Meadow to Thunder Peak (cross-country, 2½ miles)

Martin Meadow, 2 miles north of the Silver Lake spillway on Highway 88, is an excellent starting point for a climb of Thunder Peak. Green and lush, full of flowers and other plant life, it is also a fine place just to amble around in at your leisure.

Several tributaries converge just west of the highway to form the Silver Fork of the American River. Starting from a point about 200 yards south of the tributary from Thunder Peak, head southeast through the meadow and up the draw south of the spur that extends northwest from the peak. The last several hundred yards to the ridge crest are over crusty volcanic rock. Arriving at the ridge crest, follow it southeast to the summit, from which you will have fine views of Caples Lake and Silver Lake on either side.

From the peak one can descend northeast to Kirkwood Meadows or south to the Horse Canyon Trail by finding a pass through the spiny lava. Or you can follow the ridge northwest and descend along its grassy, open slopes to Carson Spur.

Sec. 1.5 Shealor Lakes (3 miles round trip)

These lakes, due west of Silver Lake, provide excellent swimming, good fishing and fair camping. The trail begins on Highway 88 1 mile south of Kaye's Resort. Heading northwest, it winds gently up for ¾ mile to a flowered and juniper-dotted ridge just south of a rocky knob (point 7689 on the topo map), from which there are fine views of the Shealor Lakes and the American River Canyon to the west, and Silver Lake to the east. From the ridge the trail descends southwest, steeply at times and with occasional switchbacks, to reach the largest of the lakes in another ¾ mile. Surrounded by granite, and fed in early season by a waterfall tumbling off the cliffs to the east, this lake is a fine spot for an afternoon picnic. The smaller lakes below are not as appealing.

Sec. 1.6 Stockton Municipal Camp to Plasse Trading Post (4 miles)

One of the early travelers on the Carson Emigrant Route was a Frenchman, recently arrived from Lyons, named Raymond Plasse. He liked what he saw in the Silver Lake area, and in 1853 he began operating a trading post on Squaw Ridge south of the lake, where the old Emigrant Route left the ridge to head west toward Mud Lake. The story is told, and confirmed to us by Plasse's grandson, that once three men staying overnight at the post learned that Plasse had considerable gold. They tortured him to force him to tell where it was. When he didn't tell, they tied him to a tree and left him; but one (the black member of the trio) relented, came back, and untied him after Plasse promised not to call the authorities for 24 hours. The men were later apprehended, but Plasse intervened on behalf of the black man, who consequently received a lighter sentence. When the road was constructed over Carson Spur, short-cutting the old route, Plasse moved to the south end of Silver Lake where, with his family, he operated a cattle ranch and resort for many years. His grandson, also Raymond Plasse, still lives there with his family in the summer, operating a more modern trading post complete with restaurant. Nothing remains of the old trading post, but the walk to it is a scenic one and full of historical echoes.

The Squaw Ridge Trail starts from a parking area 200 yards east of the Stockton Municipal Camp and proceeds south for 1½ miles to a signed junction with a trail to Hidden Lake. This portion of the route is described (in reverse) in Sec. 1.1.

Continuing south from the junction, the trail climbs moderately steeply on switchbacks up a wooded ridge and over a saddle, drops toward a large meadow, and meets a jeep road.

"What signifies knowing the names; if you know not the nature of things?" Benjamin Franklin

Turning left (east) on the jeep road, we pass Allen's Ranch on the right, then cross a series of seasonal streams, one of which carries the sign *Bear River*. These are the headwaters of the Bear River, but why this streamlet was selected for the honor, since they all flow together at the bottom of the meadow, is not clear.

About ½ mile beyond Allen's, the foot trail and the jeep road part company, the former veering off to the right and proceeding on a relatively direct, moderately steep climb up to Squaw Ridge, while the latter winds its way up a bit more circuitously and quite steeply—too steep for a vehicle without 4-wheel drive. The two routes converge at the top of Squaw Ridge, near a signed junction with the Squaw Ridge Jeep Trail. A sign just below the summit identifies the former site of Plasse Trading Post.

From the trading post site the Squaw Ridge Jeep Trail continues northeast to West Pass (Sec. 1.8), and southwest to Upper Pardoes Camp, where it meets a dirt road from Lower Bear River Reservoir. The energetic day-walker may want to hike the additional 4 miles round trip to Pardoe Lake (southwest on the jeep trail for 1¼ miles to a signed trail junction, then ¾ mile to the lake by trail) or even to make a longer loop (5 additional miles) via Cole Creek and Pardoe lakes. A jeep, of course, that will get as far as Allen's Ranch makes those lakes reachable on an easy day walk.

BACKPACK TRIPS

Sec. 1.7   Silver Lake to Summit City Canyon and . . .
(your choice)

The Horse Canyon Trail from Silver Lake to the junction with the Tahoe-Yosemite Trail in Summit City Canyon is 8¾ miles long. The first 5½ miles, from Silver Lake to Squaw Ridge, is described in Sec. 1.2. Here we describe the second segment, from Squaw Ridge down to the canyon, as a basis for any of a variety of overnight trips suggested in the subsections that follow.

From the signed junction with the Squaw Ridge Jeep Trail, the Horse Canyon Trail proceeds down moderately steep switchbacks on an open, sandy slope, crossing and recrossing a small stream bordered with Indian paintbrush, shooting stars, phlox, and wallflowers. As the trail descends it affords increasingly panoramic views. From a natural lookout point about ¾ mile down, one can see into Summit City and Mokelumne canyons and across (south) to some of the peaks beyond Kennedy Meadow, including Cooper Peak, Granite Dome and Three Chimneys.

Two switchbacks and ¼ mile from the lookout point bring you to a signed junction with a trail going southwest that leads back to the Squaw Ridge Jeep Trail at a point about 1½ miles south of the Horse Canyon Trail junction. Keeping left (southeast) at the junction, the Horse Canyon Trail descends for 1½ miles on a zigzag route through a series of small, inclined meadows. Between meadows the trail is steep and often rocky. Through the meadows, moderately forested with lodgepole and red fir, the trail is less steep and softer. Occasional grassy areas near tiny streams afford fair-to-good camp spots in the meadows.

After the last inclined meadow, the trail crosses the main stream to its east side, then leaves the main draw of Horse Canyon over a ridge to the east and plunges almost straight down a rocky route toward the canyon bottom. The terrain is mainly manzanita-covered here, with only occasional shade from an aspen or a pine, and the going tends to be difficult. Soon the steepness abates, however, and the steep zigzags turn into more sensible switchbacks for the final ½ mile as the trail approaches the canyon floor, passes through patches of wild geranium and arrives at a signed junction with the Tahoe-Yosemite Trail. Good camp spots lie near Summit City Creek in both directions.

Now what to do? You have several options:

a. *Return the way you came.* To us this option is the least desirable, both because we prefer variety and because, frankly, we dread the walk up with packs. When you come down you will see why.

b. *To Carson Pass via the Tahoe-Yosemite Trail.* This route, 7¾ miles long, provides a broad spectrum of scenery (Sec. 2.16, 2.10 and 2.8).

c. *To Forestdale Summit.* While the scenery on this route is not quite as spectacular as that in the Round Top Basin, the trip is shorter (5½ miles), the ascent more gradual, and the trail less traveled. Follow the Tahoe-Yosemite Trail north to its junction with the Summit City Trail; then take the latter to Forestdale Summit (Sec. 2.16a).

d. *To Lake Alpine.* This trip, on the Tahoe-Yosemite Trail down Summit City Canyon, across the Mokelumne, and up the other side, covers 14¾ miles from the Horse Canyon junction (Sec. 2.16, 2.17 and 3.3).

e. *The Big Loop.* If you are big on loop trails, this 35-mile trek will appeal to you. From the Horse Canyon Trail junction, take the Tahoe-Yosemite Trail south to its junction with the Munson Meadow Trail, 7¾ miles (Sec. 2.16). Then take the Munson Meadow Trail to Silver Lake (Sec. 1.10), 12½ miles. If you really want to do it right, you can leave the Munson Meadow Trail at the signed Hidden Lake junction and follow the Hidden Lake-Granite Lake Trail to Camp Minkalo (Sec. 1.1), then walk back to your starting point at the Horse Canyon trailhead.

Sec. 1.8 Horse Canyon Trail-Squaw Ridge Loop (14 miles)

We have done this loop in a single day, but we recommend at least two days in order to allow time for exploring the scenic side country. Possible overnight stops include Scout Carson

Lake, Ladeux Meadow or Upper Beebe Lake, and Horse Thief Springs.

The Horse Canyon Trail from Silver Lake to Squaw Ridge (5½ miles) is described in Sec. 1.2. Camping at or near Scout Carson Lake will enable you to visit Summit Meadow Lake and Devils Hole Lake (Sec. 1.3) as well as to climb Emigrant Peak.

From the junction of the Horse Canyon Trail and the Squaw Ridge Jeep Trail, you follow the route of the emigrant trains southwest down Squaw Ridge to the site of Plasse Trading Post (4½ miles). The jeep trail is wide, and in late season dusty, but chances are that if you go before mid-July you will be walking at least part way on snow. The earlier you go, the less likely is your peace and quiet to be disturbed by jeeps. The jeep trail climbs at first over a small promontory, providing excellent views west to Silver Lake and east to Summit City Canyon; then it descends gently and crosses Martell Flats. From these flats the ridge drops off steeply to the north; Devils Hole Lake is clearly visible, and reachable by a short but steep scramble. From a rise beyond the flats, a signed side trail (Sec. 1.9) descends to Ladeux Meadow and Beebe Lakes. About 1½ miles later the trail arrives at the site of Plasse Trading Post, and a signed junction with the jeep and foot trails to Allen's Ranch. For a discussion of Horse Thief Springs and other camp spots in the vicinity, see Sec. 1.10. The route back from Plasse Trading Post is described (in the opposite direction) in Sec. 1.6.

Sec. 1.9 Beebe Lakes Side Trip (1½ miles one way)

For years the route from the Squaw Ridge Jeep Trail to Upper Beebe Lake through Ladeux Meadow has been a designated jeep trail, the only intrusion into the wilderness area east of Squaw Ridge. It is full of ruts and rocks, and we would have considered it impassable for anything but a tank, but that's because we didn't appreciate the tenacity of jeepsters. Last time we were at Upper Beebe, an entire clubful of those friendly but noisy folk were busy setting up camp and littering the countryside.

We are pleased to report that the parcel of land southeast of Squaw Ridge, embracing Martell Flats, Ladeux Meadows, and Upper Beebe Lake, has finally been incorporated into the Mokelumne Wilderness. It may take a couple of years for the jeep-wrought devastation to disappear, but when it does this will be a delightful backpack destination.

The trail down from the signed junction with the Squaw Ridge Jeep Trail (Sec. 1.8) to Ladeux Meadow is moderately steep at first; then it levels off as it approaches the lake. Needless to say, it is a wide trail at present and easy to follow. The meadow is lovely, colorful and often full of mosquitos.

The lake itself is a jewel. Granite slopes on the north and east sides provide excellent sunbathing, and flat areas on the west and south have good campsites. When it is no longer accessible to jeeps, fishing is likely to be good as well. Lower Beebe Lake, reachable cross-country by following a series of granite ledges as they drop to the southeast, is little more than a pond in swampy terrain.

Sec. 1.10   Silver Lake to the Tahoe-Yosemite Trail via the Munson Meadow Trail (12½ miles one way)

The Munson Meadow Trail runs from Plasse Trading Post through the Mokelumne Wilderness via Munson Meadow to the Tahoe-Yosemite Trail just above Camp Irene on the Mokelumne River, 12½ miles from Silver Lake. In the area served by the northern part of the trail are a half dozen lakes, all of them within about 3 miles of Plasse Trading Post, and all of them swimmable, fishable and campable. A trip that includes one or two of them can easily be made from Silver Lake as an overnighter. All of them can be included in a trip of three days or more. Farther south, the trail provides access for an easy climb up Mokelumne Peak (Sec. 1.11[f]) and for a journey west on the Mokelumne Peak and Tanglefoot trails to Shriner Lake and Votaw Camp (Sec. 1.12). The hiker who continues down the trail to Camp Irene may climb out on the Tahoe-Yosemite Trail to Lake Alpine (Sec. 3.3) or go north up Summit City Creek to one of the northern access points to Summit City Canyon. (For a description of the Tahoe-Yosemite Trail north, see Sec. 2.16; for the Horse Canyon Trail to Silver Lake see Sec. 1.7; and for the Summit City Trail to Forestdale Summit, see Sec. 2.16).

In the section that follows this one, we describe various side routes as well. How to package these alternatives and where to stay are matters for your taste, time and condition. We begin by describing the main route.

The route from Stockton Municipal Camp to Plasse Trading Post is described as a day trip in Sec. 1.6. From the old trading-post site, the Squaw Ridge Trail runs up to the northeast and down to the southwest. About 130 yards down the Squaw Ridge Jeep Trail is a signed junction with the Munson Meadow Trail, the former continuing to the right (southwest) and the latter descending gently to the left (southeast). Signs show Long Lake to the left and Pardoe Lake to the right. The Munson Meadow Trail is itself a jeep trail at this point, and remains so until it reaches the Wilderness boundary in ½ mile.

Turning left on the Munson Meadow Trail, we arrive in about 110 yards at Horse Thief Springs. The name derives from an enterprising venture allegedly engaged in by the bandit Joaquin Murieta and his gang. The gang would steal horses from emigrants passing through on the main road, conceal them in the meadows, wait until they were freshened and fattened, and then take them over to the Nevada side and sell them to a new band of emigrants—an early form of recycling. Whether all that happened at this location is something else again. Anyway, Horse Thief Springs, which was the water source for Plasse Trading Post, gushes forth as icy cold and delicious as any you will find in the mountains. There is a good camp site nearby, though it is often used by jeepsters. Additional camp spots can be found farther down the little stream. Our trail continues south on a fairly level route to the signed Mokelumne Wilderness boundary.

From the boundary, the trail—still wide enough for jeeps at first, but no longer open to them—descends gently south along the top of a ridge. In places the terrain is heavily wooded with red fir; in others it is wide open, affording views down into Cole Creek Canyon and across to Mokelumne Peak. After about a mile the trail begins to traverse down the east side of the ridge, and in another ½ mile, partly over granite, it arrives at a signed junction with the Black Rock Lake Trail.

From the junction, our trail continues south through rolling, wooded terrain, arriving in ½ mile at a junction with a trail to Cole Creek Lakes. At the junction a gray, hard-to-spot sign reading *Cole Creek Lakes ½ mile,* is nailed 2 feet from the

Brook trout from Long Lake

bottom of a lodgepole pine about 10 yards off the trail to the right (west).

From the Cole Creek Lakes Trail junction we continue southeast down a granite slope for 100 yards, cross a stream bed (dry except in early season), climb over a small ridge with lupine, brodiaea and penstemon lining the route, and then drop steeply on a rocky slope to a small lakelet with an outlet stream that flows in early season. From here we continue to descend down the granite ridge for ¼ mile, recrossing the stream, then gradually level off and continue to a signed junction with the Long Lake Trail just over a mile from the last junction.

At the Long Lake Trail junction, the Munson Bypass trail leads right from the main trail—a short cut to Tanglefoot Canyon (Sec. 1.13). Our trail keeps left and proceeds south, nearly level at first through a small meadow, then up somewhat steeply on a duff base for ½ mile, then nearly level again on a sandy duff base through sparsely wooded terrain to Munson Meadow, and a signed junction with the Tanglefoot Trail (Sec. 1.12).

Munson Meadow is small but quite attractive. Through it runs a stream, cold in early summer. There are fair packers' campsites on the south side, and additional good camp spots farther downstream, particularly at the south end of the lower meadow, with views of Mokelumne Peak and the Mokelumne River canyon.

From Munson Meadow the Munson Meadow Trail formerly descended 4th of July Canyon to Cedar Camp (and was called the Cedar Camp trail for that reason). That old trail is now neither maintained nor traveled. The current trail, heading east, crosses the meadow stream near the packers' camp and wanders for a mile east and south over a nearly level forested plateau before it begins to descend into the canyon of the Mokelumne River. It descends gradually at first, offering fine views of the massive glacier-sculptured canyon walls. Then it drops more steeply on dusty-sandy footing down manzanita-covered slopes for about a mile.

About 2½ miles from Munson Meadow you come to what seems like an oasis in the desert—an aspen-and-alder-lined stream running through moist, fern-covered ground colored with columbine, milfoil, wild geraniums, swamp whiteheads, corn lilies and groundsel.

From the beginning of the "oasis" to the Tahoe-Yosemite Trail is about 1½ miles. The trail is a bit difficult to follow in places as it crosses and recrosses the first stream and various other streams (depending on the time of year) and wriggles its way down one spur ridge after another, steeply at times, over wet terrain, gradually entering incense-cedar and lodgepole-pine forest. The last ¼ mile is a gentle traverse to the north, then a steep descent to a junction with the Tahoe-Yosemite Trail. A right turn here takes you in ¾ mile down to Camp Irene (Sec. 2.16).

Sec. 1.11   Side Trips from the Munson Meadow Trail

a.   Black Rock Lake (1 mile)

From the signed junction with the Munson Meadow Trail (Sec. 1.10) the trail to Black Rock Lake descends east over granite slopes (colored, in season, with brilliant magenta penstemon) until it reaches the Ladeux Meadow outlet. The water here runs slowly over granite, forming pools large enough for bathing. After crossing the tributary, the trail climbs steeply east and southeast, first over duff and then over rocky terrain, to the lake. Fair-to-good campsites are found on the northeast side.

b.   From Black Rock Lake to Upper Beebe Lake (2 miles)

Ascend to the saddle east of Black Rock Lake; then continue north on the ridge, keeping to its east slope. In about ½ mile over open granite you will come to the headwaters of a tributary. Follow the stream north, ascending through three meadows. From the last meadow,

Upper Cole Creek Lake

you will spot Upper Beebe Lake in the east. Descend the moderate slope to the lake. For a description of the lake see Sec. 1.9.

c. **Cole Creek Lakes (¾ mile)**

From the signed junction with the Munson Meadow Trail (Sec. 1.10) it is a short half mile to Upper Cole Creek Lake—level at first to the west, then dropping gently to the south. The lakes are popular; if you can't find a campsite at the upper lake, continue west ¼ mile to the lower one. There are good camping and fishing at both.

d. From Pardoe Lake to Plasse Trading Post (2 miles)

From the north side of Pardoe Lake a trail traverses moderately steeply to the north, arriving in ¾ mile at a signed junction with the Squaw Ridge Jeep Trail. It is possible to walk directly up to the jeep road from the lake, but the trail is more pleasant and shorter. From the junction, the jeep road, traveling on top of the ridge most of the way, will take you to Plasse Trading Post in 1¼ miles.

e. Long Lake (1/3 mile)

From the signed junction on the Munson Meadow Trail (Sec. 1.10), the Long Lake Trail leads east over nearly level terrain, passing several ponds and arriving at the lake in 1/3 mile. There are several good camp spots and a wilderness toilet on the south side, where granite slabs jut into the water and make fine rocks for sunning after a warm swim. Some fairly large brook trout live here.

f. Mokelumne Peak (cross country)

Mokelumne Peak, at 9332 feet, is not the highest mountain in the area, but its isolated situation allows it to dominate the Mokelumne Wilderness. It can be seen from, and therefore from it can be seen, a large portion of the territory described in this book. It is, moreover, a relatively easy half-day climb from Munson Meadow, neither unduly exhausting nor particularly scary.

From Munson Meadow (Sec. 1.10), take the Tanglefoot Trail 2/3 mile to the base of the north spur of the peak. For the first ½ mile the trail descends gradually to the southwest, providing views of the peak and allowing you to plan your route. Then it descends on switchback legs west and southeast, arriving at a wide saddle running east-west over the north spur. The trail itself now descends steeply west. This is where you get off.

From the saddle you can proceed directly up the north spur, heading south, but that involves a good deal of rock scrambling. We suggest heading just east of the spur for a few hundred yards, climbing gently through a meadowy area, and then winding your way up the east side of the spur to the top of the first rocky promontory. From there, continue to climb east of the spur, crossing a runoff stream and moving toward the peak. The granitic rock here is richly patterned in shades of red and yellow; the photographer with an artistic bent will have a field day.

In a short while you will be on the rocky north spur itself. You may prefer not to walk directly on the spur, which is quite jagged, but to stay a bit east until you are nearly at the top. From the spur just below the top you can look straight down to the west at several azure ponds that lie at the base of the peak.

From the top, the 360° view is spectacular: the Crystal Range, Thunder Peak and Round Top in the north; Mt. Reba and beyond it the peaks of northern Yosemite in the south; the Mokelumne Canyon and parts of Summit City Canyon below; and across to the northeast Meadow Lake. Take your map, compass and binoculars as well as your camera.

Sec. 1.12 Munson Meadow to Tanglefoot Trailhead (11 miles)

The Wilderness area west of Mokelumne Peak is rugged, seldom traveled country with poorly graded and sometimes barely discernible trails. Its scenery is not spectacular, but it does offer isolation, quiet beauty, and an alternative route out from the southern part of the Munson Meadow Trail. About 1 mile and 400 feet of climbing can be saved by taking the cross-country shortcut south from the Long Lake Trail junction (Sec. 1.13) but doing that means missing Mokelumne Peak.

The Tanglefoot Trail from Munson Meadow to the saddle on the north spur of Mokelumne Peak is described in Sec. 1.11. From the saddle, the trail descends west, steeply at first, then levels off through a meadow where a partly obliterated sign indicates a junction with the shortcut trail to the north (Sec. 1.13).

From the junction our trail follows an undulating route around the west side of the peak for 4 miles to a small lake which has no name, so we will call it No-Name Lake. For the first ¾ mile the trail descends, steeply at times, through a dense red-fir forest. It crosses a stream and then comes to a second, larger stream with fine granite pools for bathing and good camp spots on the east side. It then climbs steeply up and over the northwest spur of Mokelumne Peak on multicolored granite underfooting, gaining nearly 1000 feet in altitude in the next 1½ miles. The trail is difficult to follow at times; keep your eye out for blazes. From the spur we begin to drop once more, now more gently, on a duff trail down a steady traverse with occasional meadows and luxuriant displays of Sierra forget-me-nots. In 1 mile from the spur we come to a marshy meadow. The trail rounds the meadow on its north side (follow the blazes) and descends to No-Name Lake, where camping is poor-to-fair.

From No-Name Lake to Shriner Lake is 3¾ miles on a singularly tortuous route from which the Tanglefoot Trail derives its name. Two long switchbacks, northward and southward, and then a series of switchbacks down the face of the ridge lead into Tanglefoot Canyon, through rich, verdant foliage fed by a multitude of small run-off streams. The trail is so wet in places that the Forest Service has installed boardwalks. A combination of luxuriant ferns and brilliantly colored flowers—paintbrush, phlox and columbine, among others—creates an almost tropical feel. As the switchbacks end, the trail descends north somewhat steeply, traversing the ridge to the forest- and fern-covered canyon floor, and crossing Tanglefoot Creek (fair-to-good camping).

From the creek, the trail climbs on short, moderate-to-steep switchbacks that lead southwest up the north side of the canyon, at first on duff through red-fir and lodgepole forest, then on a very rocky trail over glaciated granite. As the trail reaches the top of the canyon, about 1½ miles from the creek, it arrives at a junction with a trail leading north to Shriner Lake. The route to the lake is short (about ½ mile) and pleasant, winding on duff underfooting through lodgepole pine mixed with aspen, past several small ponds with the blue of Sierra forget-me-nots coloring the way. The lake is naturally beautiful, lined with granite and excellent for swimming, with fair-to-good campspots that have been somewhat overused.

From the junction with the Shriner Lake Trail, the Tanglefoot Trail heads southwest over level, heavily wooded terrain past a marshy pond, and then descends moderately steeply to the south and west over switchbacks to the trailhead on a road from Lower Bear River Reservoir. This area is heavily logged, and you may have some difficulty following the trail. Access to the Tanglefoot Trailhead is described in Section 4.1.

Sec. 1.13 Short Cut from Long Lake Trail to the Tanglefoot Trail (2 miles)

At the junction of the Long Lake and Munson Meadow trails an old, partly-maintained trail heads south-southwest, connecting with the Tanglefoot Trail at a meadow north of Mokelumne Peak. A sign reading *Votaw Camp* marks the route. It is difficult to follow in places, but for those who have had experience in finding their way about in the woods the going is fairly easy. The route ascends gradually south-southwest, passing a pond between two hills. It then descends gradually to an indistinctly signed junction with the Tanglefoot Trail.

Sec. 1.14 Silver Fork-Caples Creek Loop (7¼ miles)

The Silver Fork of the American River, which flows northwest from Silver Lake, is joined after the first quarter of its length by Caples Creek, which flows west from Caples Lake.

The two streams are separated by a ridge that culminates, near their confluence, in a large granite massif, the high point of which is marked 6927 on the topo map. From the confluence a 5¾ mile trail loop proceeds up Caples Creek, over the intervening ridge, and down the Silver Fork—an easy trip, relatively low in elevation, ideal for an early-season warm-up. It can be done easily in a single day (the total trip as we describe it is 7¼ miles) but the fishing opportunities and the variety of scenery make it attractive as a two-day venture.

Follow the mostly paved Silver Fork Road from Kyburz on US 50 southeast 10 miles to a junction with a dirt road leading east marked *Caples Creek.* Or drive to the junction from the Silver Lake area by taking a dirt road that begins at Corral Flat on Highway 88, 10 miles west of Silver Lake. (Drive 4 miles north on this road to Iron Mountain, then east on the Sherman Canyon road, following the signs to the Silver Fork.) From the junction, follow the dirt road marked *Caples Creek* east about ¼ mile and park. The road continues for another ¼ mile, but portions are difficult without 4-wheel drive. About ½ mile east of the signed junction with the Silver Fork road, the dirt road forks. Keep to the left (north). About 300 yards later the road ends and the unsigned trail begins.

At first the trail climbs somewhat steeply east, away from the stream, but in a few hundred yards it begins to level off to the southeast, passing through a dense cedar forest between the north bank of the Silver Fork and a low-lying granite ridge. After ½ mile it passes through the fence gate and follows close by the stream, arriving in another ¼ mile at the trail junction marking the west end of the loop. The unsigned trail to the left (northeast) leads up Caples Creek; the trail to the right (southeast), marked *Forgotten Flat 1, Highway 88-5,* leads up the Silver Fork. Which way you take the loop depends upon your time schedule. The better camping spots are along the Silver Fork. We will describe the loop beginning up Caples Creek.

For the first ½ mile from the signed junction, the trail follows close to the north bank of Caples Creek on a very gradual

ascent through a heavily wooded area. Then it climbs somewhat steeply for ¼ mile to the beginning of Jack Schneider
Meadow, affording fine views of the ridges that contain the
Caples Creek drainage. About ¼ mile into the meadow is a
signed trail junction, from which a trail to Cody Meadows
heads left (northeast). Our trail, signed *Highway 88-3,* heads
southeast, first fording and then gradually ascending away
from Caples Creek. After ½ mile of gradual ascent the trail
climbs moderately east for ¼ mile, and then levels off, passing
south of a small pond. From this point the trail turns abruptly
southwest, climbing up the ridge that separates Caples Creek
from the Silver Fork. After ½ mile of moderately steep to
steep climbing, the trail arrives at the top of the ridge and a
signed junction with the end of a jeep road from Highway 88.

From this junction the loop continues southwest, toward
the Silver Fork. Just where the trail begins to descend, a short
(100 yard) walk uphill to the east will bring you to a spot with
fine views east of the volcanic cliffs of Thunder Peak and of
Squaw Ridge above Silver Lake, as well as the splendid panorama of the impressive glacier-scoured granite basin that holds
the upper reaches of the Silver Fork. In early season many
waterfalls can be seen tumbling down the granite cliffs. Along
the route about ½ mile southwest is the massif labeled point
6927, from which even more impressive views can be had.
Climbing the massif is for the hardy, however; while it is not
at all dangerous, a thick ground cover of manzanita and deer
brush makes the going extremely difficult.

From the top of the ridge, the trail descends a total of 1
mile southwest to the Silver Fork. Reaching the stream, the
trail follows it at a distance of about 100 yards (several good
camp spots) passing south of the granite massif and arriving in
½ mile at a signed trail junction from which a side trail to the
left (southeast) fords the stream and continues 1½ miles to a
dirt road to Sherman Canyon.

Keeping to the right (west) our trail follows the stream on
a gradual descent through a beautiful forest of incense-cedar,

red fir and Jeffrey pine. After ¾ mile the stream begins to drop
sharply, via bubbling cataracts. Our trail follows the stream
down on moderately steep switchbacks for another ¼ mile,
then veers away to the north, curving around the contour of
the massif. In another ½ mile it levels off to cross Caples Creek
on a log and arrive back at the western end of the loop.

Section 2   Trips from the Caples Lake-Carson Pass Area

[Caples] Lake is surrounded by an amphitheatre of mountains. . . . The bases of these mountains are of granite, while their summits are breccia. Two remarkable masses of the latter rock stand forward on their granite pedestals almost into the valley, and form highly picturesque objects in a valley where all is beautiful.

Immediately on leaving the valley, our road lay up the ascent to Carson Pass proper. In rising the hill, a very fine view is obtained of [Caples] Lake Valley, with its two lakes and surrounding mountains. It is certainly the most imposing view on the road, and I believe is unsurpassed in wild beauty or grandeur by any in the state.

G. H. Goddard
Report of the Surveyor-General of California (1855)

While there have been a few changes over the last 120 years, the description remains essentially valid; and the views from the road are surpassed only by those from the mountain trails.

DAY HIKES

Sec. 2.1   Kirkwood to Lake Margaret (2 miles)

In 1864, after the road over Carson Spur was finished, Zack Kirkwood built a stage station and inn ½ mile west of the present dam on Caples Lake. When Alpine County was split from Amador, the county line went directly through the barroom, making it possible, as legend would have it, for Kirkwood to avoid tax on his cattle by moving them across the county line when the tax collector came to visit. The legal premise is dubious, but the inn is still there, providing opportunity for a bi-county beer after a hike to Lake Margaret.

From a signed trailhead on Highway 88 100 yards east of Kirkwood Inn, the trail descends north into a lovely meadow, crosses Caples Creek, and veers east for a short distance. Then it begins a gradual climb, north and then northwest, to the top of a granite ridge from which there are views back toward the Round Top range. From the top of the ridge the trail descends northwest, skirting a large pond that feeds into the North Fork Caples Creek. The trail continue northwest, following the south side of the stream downstream for ½ mile (good campspots), finally veering sharply north up a rocky slope to Lake Margaret. The walk throughout is gentle, with forest cover, making it suitable as a day outing for families with small children.

There is a fair campsite on the east side of the lake, with a pleasant view but no running water. Fishing for natural (unplanted) brook trout is good downstream on Caples Creek but the going is difficult.

Sec. 2.2   Schneider Camp to top of ridge (1 mile) or Showers Lake (2 miles)

Schneider Camp is an old cow camp acquired in part by the Forest Service for use as an overflow campground. The road to it from Caples Lake is marked most noticeably by a sign reading *Caples Lake Maintenance Station*. The road is paved for the first 1/3 mile; then, after passing through a cattle gate, it becomes dirt. About ½ mile beyond the campground, the road

arrives at an intersection with a private road leading left (south) to a cabin which is still occupied by cattlemen. The trail to the ridge and Showers Lake begins on the north side of the main road opposite this intersection.

The trail climbs gradually northeast through a luxuriant meadow which, in season, contains a lavish display of wild-flowers, comparable, we think, to the magnificent gardens on Mt. Rainier. When the flowers are blooming—usually by early July—the trip is worth it for them alone.

After ½ mile the trail climbs moderately steeply on several switchbacks for another ½ mile to the top of the volcanic ridge that extends northeast from the Carson Pass area. The view from the top is splendid: across to the east is the Carson Range, dominated by Red Lake and Stevens peaks, and be-tween the volcanic ridge you are on and the Carson Range are the magnificently verdant Meiss Meadows, dotted with numer-ous small lakes and intersected by the infant Truckee River. Round Top, the highest peak in the area, is visible to the south, usually surrounded by snow well into the summer. For even better views, climb higher on the ridge to the northwest. Adventurous hikers may want to walk cross country to the top of Peak 9595 (about 1½ miles) and back to Schneider Camp from there; the going is not at all difficult.

From the top of the ridge, the trail traverses the northeast slope of the ridge for several hundred yards, to a point from which Showers Lake can be seen directly north. It then de-scends moderately steeply for ¾ mile to the lake, where it meets the Tahoe-Yosemite Trail (Sec. 2.14).

Sec. 2.3   Carson Pass to Meiss Saddle (1 mile) or Meiss Mea-dows (2 miles); cross-country side trips.

From a trailhead on the north side of Highway 88, about 100 yards west of Carson Pass, the Pacific Crest Trail contours gently west and northwest, at first through forest cover, then through open, sandy, flower-filled terrain, arriving in ¾ mile at a junction with the "old" Meiss Meadows Trail. (The old trail, shorter but steeper, begins at a parking lot on the north side of Highway 88 0.9 mile northwest of Carson Pass.)

From the junction, the PCT climbs steeply over open slopes which provide increasingly expansive views of Round Top and its basin of lakes, as well as Caples Lake. Soon the trail meets an old jeep road, now closed to motorized travel, and climbs north on it for several hundred yards to a saddle containing a pond.

The Meiss saddle is at the southernmost part of a huge, semi-circular volcanic ridge that divides the drainages of the American and the Truckee rivers. A short walk north from the saddle (past beds of Sierra iris in mid-season) yields views of part of Lake Tahoe to the north and, west of the lake, the snowy caps of Mt. Tallac, Dicks Peak and Jacks Peak.

Meiss Ridge is itself worth exploring cross-country. You can, with a bit of extra effort, follow the ridge rather than the trail northwest to Showers Lake. Fed by snows lasting well into summer, the rich volcanic soil along the ridge nourishes a remarkably brilliant and diverse floral display, including fields of yellow mule ears, red penstemon and blue lupine, mixed with patches of paintbrush, stonecrop, groundsel and wild daisy. Here also, according to U.C. botanist Dean Taylor, can be found the Utah serviceberry, a species unreported elsewhere in the Sierra Nevada.

Northeast of the saddle is Red Lake Peak which, according to most "authorities," is the peak that General Fremont climbed on February 14, 1844, and from which he reported seeing "Lake Bigler," one of the old names for Lake Tahoe. The shortest route to the top, and the one Fremont probably followed, is straight up from what is now the Alhambra Mine, via the saddle between Red Lake Peak and Stevens Peak. Meese saddle, however, provides a more comfortable access. Follow the trail down over the saddle toward Meiss Meadows for about 200 yards, then diagonal up to the northeast. If you don't care about making the very top, you can head more east than north, ascend to the top of the ridge and then walk north on the ridge toward the peak. You will have a magnificent view, but when you are as far up as you can get, you will discover that you are separated from the very top by a substantial chasm. If you are compulsive about your peaks, then continue northeast until you are in a position to reach the ridge on the north side of the peak, and walk up from there. The last part will be a scramble.

From the Meiss saddle, the PCT descends moderately, then gently, north into the valley of the Upper Truckee River, crossing several runoff streams (dry in late season) and a westward-flowing tributary of the Truckee, and arriving in one mile at a cabin and several old barns which make up a cow camp, in the center of the valley. It is a lovely valley, full of rich, verdant meadows and tiny lakes, the surrounding volcanic rim splashed with various shades of red lichen and capped by snowy peaks. If it were in the Rocky Mountains it would be called a "park"; if it were in Switzerland it would have a hotel in the middle. On the map it has no name (we call it Meiss Meadows), and you share it only with a few other hikers and, in the meadowy portion, a goodly number of cows. It is a benign spot to wander in, or just sit and look, and some fishermen have had good luck in the shallow upper reaches of the Truckee.

Meiss Lake, to the north of the cow camp on the map, is now more of a pond surrounded by a squishy meadow.

Sec. 2.4 Caples Lake to Emigrant Lake (4¼ miles)

This trail follows much of the old Emigrant Route. The signed trail begins at the south end of the spillway at the west end of Caples Lake and follows around the lake's south side for 2¼ miles on a nearly level route. The southern lake front contains some fine sandy beaches.

Then, as the trail approaches the south end of the lake, winding past large granite boulders, it begins to climb rather steeply southward, converging upon the stream that emanates from Thimble Peak's eastern draw. After a mile of climbing, the trail arrives at a junction, from where the old Emigrant Route continues to the right and ascends to West Pass (Sec. 2.5). Turning left, our trail crosses the stream and continues to climb, with fine views back toward Caples Lake. The last part of the trail, formerly quite steep, has recently been replaced with two moderate switchbacks which bring us to the grassy meadows at the north end of Emigrant Lake.

Surrounded by granite on three sides, the lake is one of the most beautiful in the area. There are fair-to-good camp spots on the northwest side. From the northeast side a trail of use leads cross country to the saddle above 4th of July Lake (Sec. 2.11).

Sec. 2.4.1 Kirkwood Ski Area to Caples Lake Trail (3 miles)

The Kirkwood Meadows Trail may not be the most esthetically pleasing of trails, unless you happen to like ski lifts, but it does provide the shortest access to Emigrant Lake and West Pass, and it does offer the possibility of some creative semi-loop trips. (Kirkwood Ski Area to West Pass to Silver Lake, for example, is one of our favorites—about eight miles.)

The trail begins at a signed trailhead 100 yards south of the ski lodge at Kirkwood. It ascends southeast, steeply at first, then moderately, up the sparsely forested volcanic ridge that separates Kirkwood Meadows from Caples Lake. After ½ mile the trail reaches what seems like it should be the top of the ridge but isn't (the deception compensated for by fine views across the meadows to the Crystal Range) and after another ½ mile of gradual climbing meets a dirt service road that runs up the ridge from the bottom of the ski lifts. The trail follows the road upward for 100 yards, heading northeast, then crosses the road and continues in the same direction several hundred yards toward a concrete platform that serves as a placement for a recoilless rifle used for avalanche shooting. From a point just below the platform the trail jogs southeast, then south, to rejoin the road at the true ridgetop, from which there are excellent views of Caples Lake and the Round Top massif.

From the ridgetop one road follows the ridge up (south-southwest) toward the top of a chairlift. Our trail (still a road, but clearly blazed) crosses over the ridge and traverses southward down the other side. In about ¾ mile it crosses the Emigrant Trail, marked by Boy Scouts and the Forest Service, and in another ¼ mile it arrives at a clearing marked by a large green gas tank. In this area, known as Emigrant Valley, it meets the Caples Lake-West Pass Trail, described in the next section.

Sec. 2.5 Caples Lake to West Pass (5 miles)

This trip follows close to, and is often congruent with, the Carson Emigrant Route as it leads to the route's highest point. We start from Caples Lake and proceed to the Emigrant Lake junction (Sec. 2.4). From here the trail climbs somewhat steeply southwest, passing underneath the No. 4 Kirkwood Meadows chairlift in Emigrant Valley, and heading toward the first saddle southeast of Thimble Peak. From this point, about 1¼ miles from the junction, one can scale the saddle on a variety of trails of use. The official trail, however, veers southeast and ascends gently along the north slope of a hogback to a second saddle, farther southeast on the ridge, where it meets the end of the Squaw Ridge Jeep Trail. The last mile of ascent is on open, almost treeless terrain. The trail throughout this area has been partly obliterated as a result of ski activity, and is at times difficult to follow.

Sec. 2.6 Caples Lake to Silver Lake via West Pass (10½ miles)

This is an excellent trip, providing a broad variety of scenery and plant life. The trail from Caples Lake to West Pass is described in Sec. 2.5. From the pass follow the jeep road southwest for 1/3 mile to the Horse Canyon Trail and descend it to Silver Lake (Sec. 1.2).

Sec. 2.7 Woods Lake to Round Top Basin (4¼ miles)

The Round Top Basin is the most popular spot in the whole area described in this book—and little wonder. A short, easy walk takes you into magnificent alpine country with beautiful lakes, snow-capped peaks, glorious views, and lavish wildflower displays, all of them seldom equalled in areas far more remote. Like any paradise, however, its seductiveness carries the seeds of its own destruction. Most people are well-behaved in the mountains, but take enough people, have them camping around lakes on fragile meadows, add a few miscreants, and you are bound to have problems. The area remains one of singular beauty and attractiveness, but unless the government does something to protect it—and a prohibition on camping except in constructed huts or lean-tos may be the only answer— the Round Top Basin may become a campers' slum.

Meanwhile, by all means take the trip—but take it, if you will, as a day's outing. Or, if you are determined to camp, please be careful. Camp away from the lakes, use a stove rather than firewood, don't wash in the water, make your latrine far from camping spots, and carry out everything that won't burn.

The basin can be reached either from Carson Pass (Sec. 2.8) or from Woods Lake. Although a slightly steeper route, the latter is shorter and less travelled, allowing an attractive half-day loop without a retracing of steps.

The trailhead is on the road to Woods Lake about 100 yards north of the lake, marked by a sign reading *Woods Lake Trail*. After crossing the outlet on a log, the trail continues east (avoid another trail that leads downstream) and begins to climb east of the lake under a forest cover of red fir and hemlock, through a series of small meadows containing various shades of phlox, thousands of buttercups, and many shooting stars.

In a short ½ mile you come upon a relic of the mining period—a huge circular stone, 10 feet in diameter, set in a hole. Called an "arrastre," it was a crushing device first used by Mexican miners for pulverizing gold or silver ore.

After passing the arrastre the trail leaves the forest and begins a steady climb up the creek to Winnemucca Lake. Views of the soaring Round Top crest ahead, and the changing colors at your feet (mule ears, paintbrush and Sierra forget-me-nots, among other flowers, line the trail) should be enough to keep your mind off any thoughts of fatigue. A final climb over generally dry terrain near the top brings you in 1½ miles to Winnemucca Lake.

This lake sits in a basin fringed with whitebark pine and mountain hemlock, bounded on the south by the massive rampart of Round Top Peak and on the east by hulking Elephants Back. The latter is an easy climb up the south flank and, though Central Valley smog may prevent your seeing as far as Kit Carson did, the view of the surrounding lakes and peaks is excellent. Winnemucca Lake's northwest shore provides fair-to-good but usually crowded camping. If you are camping overnight, we suggest the meadows below Round Top Lake.

At Winnemucca Lake our trail joins the Tahoe-Yosemite Trail coming from Carson Pass and, after crossing the lake's outlet, traverses gently eastward and upward on an open slope to a shallow saddle, with a glimpse of Lake Tahoe along the way. On the saddle in mid-season can be found specimens of rockfringe, a low-growing, very striking, red-purple flower. From the saddle the trail descends gently through sagebrush and red mountain heather to Round Top Lake.

Round Top Lake has much to offer. Towering above it to the southeast is its namesake mountain, at 10,380 feet the highest elevation in this book, and several smaller peaks known as the Round Top sisters. On its north side Round Top usually bears snow into late summer. It can be climbed, however, by the route described in Sec. 2.9. On the lake's north side is a grassy ledge that drops off rather sharply, affording open vistas.

On the north side of the lake is a signed trail junction where the Tahoe-Yosemite Trail continues east to 4th of July Lake, and our route descends northwest toward Lost Cabin Mine.

Keeping to the east side of the meadowy valley (worth a side
trip even if you're not camping there), the trail descends moderately for a short ¼ mile to a stream and then follows the
stream as it curves northward through the lower part of the
valley. The route then descends steeply north-northeast down
a rocky slope through a moderate forest cover of lodgepole
pine and hemlock, arriving in 1¼ miles from Round Top Lake
at the Lost Cabin Mine and a junction with a dead-end road.
Though the mine is abandoned, some of the old buildings, the
mine shaft, and a trestle still remain. The trailhead here is unsigned; if you are starting from Lost Cabin Mine, pass under
the trestle and climb east a few yards to the trail. The road
down from Lost Cabin Mine leads ¼ mile to the main Woods
Lake dirt road and from there it is a short ¼ mile south to the
point where you began.

Sec. 2.8   Carson Pass to Round Top Basin (3¼ miles)

From the parking lot at Carson Pass (there is additional
parking downhill to the east), the heavily trafficked route to the
Round Top Basin contours south-to-southwest through a
meadowy silver- and lodgepole-pine forest, then climbs gently
east, arriving in ¾ mile at Frog Lake. In the large patch of
sagebrush near the west end of the lake, look for the fascinat-
ing rattleweed, with its inflated, rattlelike fruits.

About 200 yards south of Frog Lake the trail to Winnemucca Lake leaves the Pacific Crest Trail (Sec. 2.13) and
ascends gently southward along the west flank of Elephants
Back, colored with patches of monkey flower and willow-herb,
then levels off, arriving at the lake in just under 2 miles. The
light-to-moderate forest cover along the way is predominantly
whitebark pine and mountain hemlock, in contrast to the silver
and lodgepole pine of the pre-Frog Lake elevations. The trail
from Winnemucca Lake to Round Top Lake is described in
Sec. 2.7.

Sec. 2.9 Climbing Round Top Peak

On August 17, 1863, the famous botanist, William H. Brewer, climbed Round Top Peak and described what he saw:

> The last 800 or 1000 feet rise in a steep volcanic mass, so steep as to be accessible in only one place, but there was no serious difficulty or danger. . . . Lake [Tahoe] was in full view its whole extent. . . . I am higher than the great crest of the Sierra here and hundreds of snowy peaks are in sight. Hope Valley lies beneath, green and lovely—high mountains, 11,000 feet high, rising beyond it. Besides Lake Tahoe there are ten smaller lakes in sight, from two miles long down to mere ponds (which were not counted)—all blue, of clear snow water. It was, indeed, a grand view.

Since his description of the view from the top can hardly be improved upon, we have only to tell you how to get there. A well-worn path begins at the east end of Round Top Lake and climbs steeply to the saddle west of the summit block. The view of Round Top Lake from here will make clear why it was originally called Sock Lake. Turning east (left) at the saddle, the trail proceeds up the pinnacle toward the peak. The last few yards are steep and rather hairy. If you don't feel like doing them (and you shouldn't, if you're not sure of your footing) don't feel bad: you can see just about everything Brewer saw anyway.

Sec. 2.10 Woods Lake or Carson Pass to 4th of July Lake

The easiest round-trip route to 4th of July Lake is from Forestdale Summit (Sec. 2.17). Those who want to enjoy the Round Top Basin on the way, however, may walk to Round Top Lake from either Woods Lake (Sec. 2.7) or Carson Pass (Sec. 2.8). From there to 4th of July Lake is 1¾ miles.

From the junction with the Lost Cabin Mine Trail near the outlet of Round Top Lake (Sec. 2.7) the Tahoe-Yosemite Trail curves around the northwest shoulder of Round Top, affording fine views east to Markleeville Peak and north to Hawkins Peak and the Crystal Range. Rounding the shoulder, the trail descends to a saddle ¾ mile from Round Top Lake which marks both the border of the Mokelumne Wilderness and the divide between the American River watershed on the north and the Mokelumne River watershed on the south.

From the saddle, the Forest Service has constructed a new trail, which switchbacks down the east side of the watershed to the lake. While moderately steep, it is a considerable improvement over the older, kamikaze route which followed the fall line.

4th of July Lake is a very special place—among other attractions it has a sandy beach above which is a small grassy plateau shaded by two handsome silver pines—but it is on that account very popular. The Wilderness Ranger asks (and we ask) that if you camp here, you camp away from the water and use a stove rather than firewood.

4th of July Lake

Sec. 2.11 From 4th of July Saddle to Emigrant Lake
(cross country, 1¼ miles)

From the saddle north of 4th of July Lake described in
Sec. 2.10 there is an easy cross-country route to Emigrant
Lake, which makes possible a variety of loop trips that we
leave to your imagination. From the Wilderness Boundary sign
at the saddle, look west toward Thimble Peak and you will see
a notch in the ridge in front of you directly in line with the
center of the peak. Proceed to that notch, either by maintaining a level contour or, depending upon snow conditions, by
dropping down into the intervening valley and then climbing
back up. Over that notch you will find a gully that leads
directly to Emigrant Lake, several hundred yards below to the
west. If you are eastbound from the lake, the trail of use up
the gully is readily discernible.

Sec. 2.12 From 4th of July Saddle to West Pass
(cross country, 2 miles)

This is a handy 2-mile cross-country link between the
Tahoe-Yosemite Trail and the various trails that connect at
West Pass. Using it, one can, for example, travel from either
Carson Pass or Woods Lake past Round Top Lake and the 4th
of July Saddle (Sec. 2.7, 2.8) over to West Pass, and then to
either Silver Lake via the Horse Canyon Trail (a total of 11¾
miles) or down to Caples Lake via the Emigrant Route (a total
of 11¼ miles). And one can see some beautiful country in the
process. Though rocky and a bit steep in places, the route requires no special equipment or climbing skill, except in early
season when an ice axe and even a rope (plus a knowledge of
how to use them) would be handy over the open, snowy slopes.

When the snow is gone, the route is clearly visible from the
saddle as it climbs steeply up the hill to the west. The hill is
open and generally dry, with little in the way of plant life
except for an occasional wild geranium, a few columbines and
penstemons, and patches of phlox. As you climb, you begin to

get views southeast to Little Indian Valley, Wet Meadows, and Raymond and Reynolds peaks beyond. Instead of going directly to the top of the crest, the route contours around the north side to a kind of saddle where there is a small meadow full of paintbrush, phlox and mule ears. The route proceeds west up the ridge, keeping just below the top on the south side, until it reaches the cliffs above Emigrant Lake. (To get to Emigrant Lake from here, simply walk down the spur to the north until you reach a walkable gully to the west; this is an alternative to the cross-country route described in Sec. 2.11.)

From the cliffs above Emigrant Lake, our route veers south, following up the ridge, but keeping just to the east side of the top. The climb is moderate at first, then fairly steep on a ducked route, partly over talus, leading to the top of the unnamed peak just northeast of Emigrant Peak. You have a clear view down into 4th of July Lake all the way, and from the top a view of Mokelumne Peak to the south and the entire Sierra Crest beyond. The route then dips down to the saddle and up to Emigrant Peak, through meadowy fields of sage colored by unusually small penstemon and patches of white phlox and blue flax. From the top of Emigrant Peak, with its microwave station, we have additional views down into Summit City Canyon and over to Silver Lake and Thimble and Thunder peaks.

From Emigrant Peak it is a short, easy walk down to West Pass (9560'), which a metal sign advises us is the highest point reached by covered wagon in the United States. The same sign asserts that on a clear day the Coast Range can be seen. We have no reason to disbelieve either assertion.

Sec. 2.13 Pacific Crest Trail from Carson Pass to Forestdale Summit (4½ miles)

This segment of the Pacific Crest Trail, recently constructed and moderately graded throughout, provides breathtaking views, magnificent flora, and opportunity for a variety of loop trips. From Forestdale Summit, for example, you can proceed to 4th of July Lake (Sec. 2.16), then back to Carson Pass via the Round Top Basin (Sec. 2.10).

The first mile of the trail, from Carson Pass to Frog Lake, is described in Section 2.8. From a signed junction 200 yards south of Frog Lake, the trail ascends southeast, toward Elephants Back; then, in 1/8 mile it veers east and climbs to the pachyderm's flank, from which there are fine views of Caples Lake and the Round Top basin to the west, and across Hope Valley to Markleeville Peak and the aptly named Nipple, to the east. The summit of Elephants Back, which provides an even broader panorama, is climbable from here but more accessible from the south.

From the flank of Elephants Back the trail descends southeast, traversing the steep northeast slope of the mountain, with an occasional switchback, to a point almost due east of the summit. This part of the trail is likely to contain a good deal of snow well into the summer, and you may have to pick your own way. An ice axe, when the snow is heavy, would be useful.

From the point almost due east of the summit, the trail descends northeast to a granite knob, then south and east again to another, more pointed knob overlooking the Forestdale Creek drainage. This is lush, meadowy country with magnificent floral displays in season.

The trail circumvents the pointed knob, then descends, first southwest and then south, partly on switchbacks, to the flowered headwaters of Forestdale Creek. It crosses the western tributary (an intermittent stream, but still a wet prospect in early season), climbs in a series of switchbacks to the south, then veers west and, remaining nearly level, crosses the main stream just below a small pond. Continuing west, the trail passes a second pond, and then begins a steady climb on switchbacks, first southeast, then southwest, then southeast again, until it joins the Summit City Trail 100 yards from Forestdale Summit.

OVERNIGHT TRIPS

Sec. 2.14   Showers Lake-Schneider Camp Semi-Loop
(9 miles)

For a trip that can be done comfortably in two days this is one of our all-time favorites. The scenery is beautiful, the walking is easy, there is ample opportunity for cross-country side trips, and in season (usually mid-July to mid-August) the wildflowers are spectacular.

The first leg of the journey, from Carson Pass to Showers Lake (4½ miles) is part of the Tahoe-Yosemite Trail. The trail begins at a parking lot on the north side of Highway 88, 1/3 mile northwest of Carson Pass. Rocky and dusty at times, the trail ascends gently west through a moderate forest cover of red fir, lodgepole pine and occasional clumps of aspen. After rounding the nose of a ridge, the trail crosses a runoff stream and then climbs over open slopes which provide views to the south of Round Top Peak and its basin of lakes. Soon the trail meets an old jeep road, now closed to motorized travel, and climbs north on it for several hundred yards to a saddle containing a pond.

The saddle is at the southernmost part of a huge, semicircular volcanic ridge that divides the drainages of the American and Truckee rivers. In the north is Lake Tahoe, partly visible, and to its west the snowy caps of Mt. Tallac, Dicks Peak and Jacks Peak. Along the volcanic ridge immediately northeast are Red Lake and Stevens peaks, both easily climbable by cross-country walking. You can, though with a bit of extra effort, follow the ridge rather than the trail northwest to Showers Lake. Fed by snows lasting well into summer, the rich volcanic soil along the ridge nourishes a remarkably brilliant and diverse floral display, including fields of yellow mule ears, red penstemon and blue lupine, mixed with patches of paintbrush, stonecrop, groundsel and wild daisy. Here also, according to U.C. botanist Dean Taylor, can be found the Utah serviceberry, a species unreported elsewhere in the Sierra Nevada.

From the saddle, the trail descends moderately, then gently, into the valley of the Upper Truckee River. It is a lovely valley, full of rich, verdant meadows and tiny lakes, the surrounding volcanic rim splashed with varying shades of red lichen and capped with snowy peaks. If it were in the Rocky Mountains it would be called a "park"; if it were in Switzerland it would have a hotel in the middle. Here it has no name, and you share it only with other backpackers and, in the meadowy portion, a goodly number of cows. After crossing several runoff streams (dry in late season) and a westward-flowing tributary of the Truckee, you pass several old cow barns and a cabin used by stockmen. Just beyond, a trail branches right to Round Lake (Sec. 2.14[a]). Our route continues north as a level jeep road through the valley, crossing the headwaters of the Truckee on boulders. Just beyond the ford a jeep road turns right (northeast) to Meiss Lake. Keeping left, our route continues north-

cow camp on Upper Truckee River

west to the edge of the meadows. From here, at a point marked by an "S" blaze on a lodgepole pine, a short-cut stockmen's route leads over the ridge 1½ miles to Schneider Camp, affording spectacular views of the immediate area as well as of the Dardanelles in the south and the Desolation Wilderness area and Lake Tahoe in the north.

From the west edge of the meadows, the trail climbs gently over a small ridge bordering Dixon Canyon, descends past a small pond and, rejoining the closed jeep road, crosses two runoff streams (fair-to-good camping) and begins to climb, steeply at times, through a forest of silver and lodgepole pine, red fir and hemlock. It emerges after ¼ mile onto a sloping meadow covered with lupine and mule ears. Sixty yards into the meadow, the trail and the road part company. The trail traverses up a colorful, meadowy bowl to a saddle above the southeast side of Showers Lake, where it meets the jeep road once more. From here you descend to the deep lake, which has good campsites on the southeast and northeast sides. Four Lakes, about one mile due east, are shallower and therefore likely to be warmer for swimming, but getting to them involves about 400 feet of climbing.

Our route continues from the west side of Showers Lake, heading first west toward the jagged volcanic palisades which jut out from the main ridge, then veering north and traversing up and around a large, magnificent open bowl. Fed by runoff streams from snow cornices which last well into summer, and often snowy itself into midseason, the bowl is a big garden of flowers, water, and glacially polished granite, sufficient to challenge any amateur naturalist and delight any photographer. Columbine and larkspur, monkey flower and penstemon, alpine lily and mountain bluebell, aster and corn lily, mule ears—they're all there, and more.

After ascending to the northwest rim of the bowl and passing through a fence, the trail levels off and heads north through a willow-covered meadow, arriving in ¾ mile at a signed junction where the trail continuing north goes to Echo Summit and we turn west toward Schneider Camp (see *The Tahoe Sierra* for descriptions of trails between here and Lassen National Park). After climbing gently up and over a spur that extends north from Peak 9595, we descend through lightly wooded terrain to the bottom of the draw between the north and west spurs. Here we find another flower garden, not quite so lavish as the last. After crossing the stream that runs through the draw, we ascend the western spur and then level off, following the contour south for 1 mile to the ridge of the southwest spur, with views of Horsetail Falls and Desolation Valley in the northwest. After passing through a fence gate, we descend sharply south through a magnificent meadowy bowl, containing a floral display even more spectacular than those previously described, and arrive at the Schneider Camp road. A left turn leads to Schneider Camp, now operated by the Forest Service as a rustic spillover car camp for the Caples Lake area. (A shorter semiloop can be made using the trail from Showers Lake described in Sec. 2.2).

Sec. 2.14(a) Side Trip to Round Lake (2 miles)

From a junction with the PCT at the cow camp in Meiss Meadows (see sec. 2.3) the trail to Round Lake heads north-northwest on an undulating route through a red-fir and lodgepole-pine forest, crossing two runoff streams (dry in late season), both surrounded by grassy, flower-filled meadows. Beyond the second stream, after a brief and gentle climb, the trail descends north along the base of the northwest spur of Stevens Peak, then drops steeply down a rocky, eroded path to Round Lake. There are fair-to-good camp spots on the lake's north shore and on the plateau above the south shore. The trail continues north from the lake, descending through a red-fir and lodgepole-pine forest to arrive at Highway 89 in about 3 miles.

Sec. 2.15 Carson Pass or Woods Lake to Forestdale Summit via 4th of July Lake (9½ miles shuttle)

This 9½ mile shuttle trip from Carson Pass (slightly less

from Woods Lake) can be done in a day, but since it involves a good deal of elevation change and passes through country that deserves more time, we suggest you allow at least two days, camping overnight either at 4th of July Lake or in Summit City Canyon. Taking in both Round Top Basin and the upper portion of Summit City Canyon, it provides a fine sampling of the many scenic contrasts that abound in the area. The whole route is described elsewhere in this book. Proceed to Round Top Lake from either Carson Pass (Sec. 2.8) or Woods Lake (Sec. 2.7), then over the saddle and down to 4th of July Lake (Sec. 2.10); then down the Tahoe-Yosemite Trail to its junction with the Summit City Canyon Trail (Sec. 2.16[b]) and then up the Summit City Trail to Forestdale Summit (Sec. 2.16[a]).

Sec. 2.16   Summit City Canyon: From Forestdale Summit or Carson Pass to the Mokelumne

Through the centuries the waters of Summit City Creek, flowing and tumbling down from Forestdale Summit to the Mokelumne River, have carved a wondrous canyon, rich in scenery and historical interest. It is also, we feel compelled to disclose, somewhat rich in rattlesnakes, so be careful.

There are three access routes to Summit City Canyon from the north. The longest is the Horse Canyon Trail from Silver Lake; the shortest and easiest (never more than 10% in grade) is the Summit City Trail from Forestdale Summit; the most scenic, but also the busiest, is the Tahoe-Yosemite Trail from Carson Pass via 4th of July Lake. We have described elsewhere the Horse Canyon Trail (Sec. 1.7); here we describe the two shorter routes to the intersection of those two routes in Summit City Canyon (sections 2.16[a] and 2.16[b]), and from that intersection down Summit City Creek to the Mokelumne (Sec. 2.16[c]). For description of the route from the confluence of Summit City Creek and the Mokelumne down-river to Camp Irene, and from Camp Irene to Salt Springs Reservoir, see sections 2.17 and 3.4.

Sec. 2.16(a)   From Forestdale Summit to Summit City Canyon (3½ miles)

Forestdale Summit, at the top of the Blue Lakes-Red Lake road, is accessible from Red Lake on Highway 88, but only by a steep and rutty road most suitable for vehicles with 4-wheel drive. If you have an ordinary passenger car we recommend the longer access, south from Highway 88 at Hope Valley to Lower Blue Lake, then back north past Upper Blue Lake to the summit. The first sign you see near the summit, 2½ miles from Upper Blue Lake, marks the jeep road down Summit City Creek. Avoid it for hiking: it is steep, dusty, rutty, and generally uncomfortable. The trailhead is a few yards beyond, marked by a sign reading *Summit City Creek 3; 4th of July Lake 7.*

The upper part of the trail gives you that "top-of-the-world" feeling: the towering granite dome to the north-northwest is Elephants Back, and directly to the west is Round Top. To the south, farther away, is Mt. Reba; closer by and below the trail are the headwaters of Summit City Creek.

From the top, the trail proceeds west-southwest, which is its overall direction. After ¼ mile it makes a brief jog east, then resumes its course, traversing the upper part of an inclined meadow that extends nearly down to the creek. The wet volcanic soil here produces a profusion of colorful flowers in early and mid season: paintbrush, lupine, wild geranium, larkspur, groundsel, corn lily, Sierra forget-me-not, phlox, aster—you name it. Only 100 yards after crossing a small stream on wooden slats is a signed junction with the Evergreen Trail from Upper Blue Lake. The meadow along upper Summit City Creek offers good camping or an attractive destination for a one-day outing.

The trail continues its traverse for nearly ½ mile to a rocky slope, makes a short jog east, and resumes its prevailing direction without interruption for nearly 1½ miles, descending gradually on rocky, then dusty, underfooting over open slopes just above treeline. To the west you can see the ledge on which 4th of July Lake sits, and its outlet stream. The massive granite prominence to the south, though its summit is over 9600 feet, has no name on the map. Down its sheer north-facing wall numerous waterfalls plunge in early season.

After 1½ miles of flirtation with timberline, the trail now enters a red-fir forest which provides both softer footing and welcome shade. After two switchbacks to the east—the first for ¼ mile to a dry gully, the second one much shorter—the trail begins to level off as it approaches the canyon floor. About ½ mile west is the signed border of the wilderness area. An old privy and the jeep trail lie only a few yards to the south, and the stream about 100 yards beyond. About 100 yards west of the wilderness boundary sign, the Summit City Trail joins the Tahoe-Yosemite Trail from 4th of July Lake (Sec. 2.16[b]).

Sec. 2.16(b)   From Carson Pass to Summit City Canyon (6¼ miles)

The route from Carson Pass to 4th of July Lake is described in sections 2.8 and 2.10. From the lake's outlet, the Tahoe-Yosemite Trail descends 650 feet into Summit City Canyon on a gentle-to-moderate eastward traverse, joining the Summit City Canyon trail in 1¼ miles. There is a sparse forest cover of red fir, lodgepole pine and silver pine near the lake, but it soon disappears, and the open slopes provide fine views of the canyon's steep granite walls. As we near the canyon floor, the sandy trail re-enters a sparse red-fir and lodgepole-pine forest with a ground cover of sagebrush, snowbrush, creamberry and spiraea, meeting the Summit City Canyon Trail at a point about 100 yards west of the Wilderness Boundary.

Sec. 2.16(c)   Down Summit City Canyon: from trail junction to the Mokelumne (4 miles)

From its junction with the Summit City Canyon Trail as described in the preceding section, the Tahoe-Yosemite Trail veers away from the stream over generally sandy terrain dotted with sagebrush and lodgepole pine, and then contours around the upper edge of a grassy meadow. In the wetter parts of the meadow wild onion, with its 6-petaled purple-and-white flowers, grows in profusion. In ¼ mile the trail begins to veer back toward the stream, and in another ¼ mile it arrives at the stream by some good-to-excellent campsites. The trail follows the stream closely now in its still gentle course down the canyon. Soon it meets and crosses the 4th of July Lake outlet, which contains numerous small waterfalls, and in about ½ mile it encounters a sign which reads *Lower Summit City 1862–1867.* Whether this was in fact the exact site of the once prosperous rival of Summit City proper is conjectural.

The trail continues its gradual descent, looping several times away from the stream and back again on soft terrain through

Summit City Creek in trailless area

lodgepole pine, aspen and willow—an altogether pleasant walk that brings you, in two miles from the Lower Summit City sign, to a signed junction with the Horse Canyon Trail (Sec. 1.7). Continuing on, our trail crosses Horse Canyon Creek and then follows close to the main stream. The canyon narrows now, and the stream flows over huge granite slabs which contain numerous pools both bathable and fishable. The trail descends gradually over sandy terrain, through a forest of baby firs. A sign ½ mile from the last junction calls our attention to a rocky draw to the west called "Telephone Gulch," the location of an old telephone ground line which connected PG&E installations on the lower Mokelumne with those at Blue Lakes. The cliffs on both sides get steeper, those on the east bearing numerous waterfalls in early season. Fern and aspen line the trail, providing a lush, green contrast to the towering, bare gray granite. A mile from Telephone Gulch is a packer's camp (good camping) and ½ mile beyond it is a sign marking Grouse Creek to the east. About 100 yards beyond this sign is a fine-but-illegal campsite by a sandy beach.

Until a few years ago, this campsite marked the end of the trail, and the trip to the Mokelumne was over a difficult cross-country route. For good or for worse, depending upon your point of view, the Forest Service has cleared and marked the route as a "trailway," shortening it in the process, and making it far more accessible to backpackers. The rattlesnakes, however, remain: our last trip down the canyon and reports from others tend to support the canyon's nickname: Rattlesnake Gulch.

From what used to be trail's end (about 1½ miles below Telephone Gulch) the trailway continues on the west bank of the creek for ½ mile over granite to a log crossing (100 yards after you leave the granite). Crossing the creek, the trailway follows close to the east bank, never more than 100 yards away from the stream. Passing first through a small burn area (believed to be the product of a careless camper's fire) the trailway proceeds again over granite, traversing just below and to the creekside of two small granite domes, then ascending a promontory (dubbed "Snag-Your-Eyeballs Point" by Wilderness Ranger Woody Hesselbarth) with magnificent views down to the Mokelumne River canyon. From the promontory, the trailway descends, steeply at first, then moderately, to an open granite bench, clearly identifiable as a large, almost flat spot on the topo map, from which you can see Summit City Creek as well as the Mokelumne River canyon. Upon crossing the granite bench to the stream, you will find lovely granite-lined bathing pools below a cataract, and a sandy beach for picnicking, camping or just plain napping.

The next segment, which brings you to the floor of the river canyon, is considerably easier. It includes three small loops away from the stream and back again, the stream being never more than 200 yards away. The first loop starts about

Mokelumne River above Camp Irene

1/8 mile downstream from the pools just described, veers away from the stream over a small promontory, and then descends steeply back to streamside. Then the route follows close to the stream for ¼ mile before the second loop, which takes you sharply to the east-southeast over a ridge, then zigzags steeply down its south side back to the stream. Then the route veers away for the last time, heading east; but since the stream itself soon veers east, it is only a few hundred yards until route and stream meet again.

Several hundred yards downstream from this point, the stream branches into two distributaries, each flowing into the Mokelumne River in about ¼ mile. Our route, however, crosses the stream on a large, barkless dead tree, traverses southeast up the opposite bank, and continues south 50 yards to an un-signed junction in a sandy flat. Between the distributaries is a rocky-sandy delta which provides fair-to-good camping.

Sec. 2.17　The Tahoe-Yosemite Trail from Summit City Creek to Camp Irene (2¼ miles)

This part of the Tahoe-Yosemite Trail, like the part through Summit City Canyon, has become converted from a cross-country route into a well-blazed, well-used thoroughfare. From the sandy flat described in the last paragraph of the preceding section, the trail heads southeast for 1/8 mile, then veers southwest, traverses a granite slope, and descends gently through a dense forest, maintaining a distance of several hundred yards from the river. About a mile from the sandy flat, the trail turns south and climbs moderately steeply to a junction with the Munson Meadow trail. (See Sec. 1.10.) From the junction it is about ½ mile of easy scampering down to Camp Irene. The last few yards cross a small burn area, the product of a 1974 fire, which is recovering nicely thanks to some young white pines. Camp Irene is a lovely spot with a sandy beach, granite slabs, and beautiful pools along the river. It gets a lot of use, however, and the use shows. If you camp, camp lightly.

Section 3   Trips from the Ebbetts Pass Road (Highway 4)

There is much beautiful scenery north of the Ebbetts Pass Road, between it and the trails described elsewhere in this book, which you can discover on your own by cross-country walks. The *trails* from that direction, however, are relatively few in number. We describe them here without regard to distinctions between one-day and overnight trips.

Sec. 3.1   Wheeler Lake

The trail begins 1.7 miles east of the Lake Alpine resort at a small parking area off the north side of the road. It is signed, but the sign is not visible from the road.

The trail climbs moderately at first, going north-northwest through a forest of red fir and lodgepole pine, with a smattering of silver pine, then continues north through an open basin and proceeds steeply up to the top of a ridge. Near the top there are occasional junipers and Jeffrey pines, but the trail is mostly unshaded and, given its southern exposure and lack of water, it is best travelled during a cool part of the day. About ½ mile up the trail, and again about 50 yards below the ridge top, there are unsigned and little used trails leading off to the right (east). The trip to the ridge is unusually scenic, affording open vistas to the south of Lake Alpine and the Spicer Meadow and Utica reservoirs, as well as of The Dardanelles and Dardanelles Cone. The ridge itself is imposing, with jagged lava pinnacles protruding on the western side. From the top you get views of Mokelumne Peak and Round Top to the northeast, and of Hawkins and Freel peaks in the distance to the north. At the top of the ridge is a junction from which Underwood Valley is ½ mile straight ahead and Wheeler Lake and Cat Valley are to the right.

The trail follows the ridge northeast for ¼ mile, reaching its crest at a notch between a lava promontory on the left and a granite knob on the right. Wheeler Lake is visible from the top of the knob, and partly visible from farther down the trail. Just below the lava are colorful displays of rock fringe and whorled penstemon.

After descending north for ¼ mile, steeply at first, over eroded, dusty terrain, the trail veers east and traverses the lower part of a large, grassy bowl on the north side of the lava ridge we crossed. The volcanic rock to the east is marvelously colorful, with hues ranging from bright reds to yellows and near-blacks. After crossing a small stream on the west side of the bowl, the trail continues to descend somewhat steeply for ½ mile across the bowl to its east side, arriving at a second stream, the main inlet of Wheeler Lake. Here a trail takes off across the stream and continues east to Sandy Meadows.

Our trail continues north down the west side of the stream for a short distance, then veers west and north again, descending moderately to reach Wheeler Lake in ½ mile. Wheeler Lake is rather shallow but with good swimming, sometimes good fishing for brook trout (8–12 inches) and fair-to-good campsites on its south and north shores.

Sec. 3.2 Wheeler Lake-Frog Lake Loop (9 miles)

From Wheeler Lake to Frog Lake the trail, though misleadingly signed in places, is well blazed and clearly visible. Starting from the side of Wheeler Lake, it climbs gently north for a short ½ mile to a Y junction where a dim trail continues straight, in the direction of Jackass Canyon. Our trail, to the left, climbs steeply northwest and then traverses less steeply north up a ridge dominated by the Peak 8885 on the map, arriving in ¾ mile at what seems to be a three-way signed junction. Actually the trail to the right, marked *Frog Lake,* and the trail to the left, marked *Underwood Valley,* both fade out in a short distance. Our trail to Frog Lake continues straight ahead, traversing northwest and shortly topping the northeast spur of Peak 8885, from which one has views into Jackass Canyon and

Cat Valley. (A new topographic map, under final preparation by the U.S. Geological Survey, indicates this peak is 50 feet lower than it was originally mapped. Although USGS has more rigid standards than most map makers, it is, nevertheless, human, and its maps contain dozens of errors.)

The trail descends from the spur, gently at first and then steeply down its western side, levels off on granite slabs at the top of a large meadow, crosses a stream, and arrives at a sign stating simply *Cat Valley*. About 200 yards west of the sign is the junction where the sign belongs. The trail straight ahead continues to Underwood Valley; the trail to the right heads north along the meadow for about 1/8 mile, then veers west over a small ridge and in another ¼ mile descends to Frog Lake. This lily-filled lake, bordered by meadows on its east side, has fair campsites on the west.

From the previous trail junction, the trail to Underwood Valley traverses gently west, then gradually southwest, crosses a shallow saddle between Peaks 8885 and 8354, and a short distance thereafter passes through a stock fence and heads down into Underwood Valley. The route descends south rather steeply at first, then gradually levels off and veers southeast, so that soon it is descending very gently on a bench. With the green valley below, the light granite cliffs directly above, and the dark lava cliffs in the distance, this part of the trip is extremely attractive. After about 1 mile the trail begins to descend toward the stream, and if you were to follow the main trail all the way you would end up crossing the stream and heading toward a cabin on the west side of the valley. If your objective is to get back to Wheeler Lake, however, or to the ridgetop junction on the Wheeler Lake Trail, you want to stay on the east side of the valley and lose as little elevation as possible.

One alternative you have is to proceed cross country, heading for the saddle southwest of Wheeler Lake (on a direct line between the numbers "27" and "28" on the topo map), and drop down to the lake from there. The other is to follow the main trail down toward the stream until, in several hundred yards, you come upon a blazed trail to the left (east). This trail, very indistinct in places, leads southeast, crosses the upper part of Underwood Valley, and switchbacks up the steep north slope of the main east-west ridge, arriving finally on the ridgetop at a signed junction with the Wheeler Lake Trail (Sec. 3.1).

Sec. 3.3   Lake Alpine to Camp Irene (7½ miles)

This segment of the Tahoe-Yosemite Trail provides the shortest access to the Mokelumne River canyon, but the 3500-foot elevation loss going in has to be strenuously regained coming out, whether you retrace your steps or go on to Silver Lake.

The Tahoe-Yosemite Trail leaves Highway 4 northbound at the Chickaree Picnic Ground at the east end of Lake Alpine, but the walk is shorter if one begins at the end of a 1/3-mile-long road that serves a summer home tract in Bee Gulch on the lake's north shore. This road leaves the highway 1/3 mile east of Lake Alpine Resort. From road's end we follow a blazed trail north, under a moderate forest cover of mixed conifers. Just before this route crosses the Bee Gulch stream, the Tahoe-Yosemite Trail comes in on the right. Beyond the ford our gentle climb increases to moderate as the rocky trail leads north under a dense canopy of lodgepole and red fir. Then, about a mile from the road, in the shade of a tall lodgepole, the trail forks. The right fork refords the stream, bound for Wheeler Lake. Our fork, the left one, climbs moderately, sometimes steeply north-northwest, under red fir and silver pine, passing through a corner of the *Big Meadow* quadrangle for about ½ mile. At the lowest saddle on the north-south divide in the very southeast corner of the *Silver Lake* quadrangle, the trail meets a dirt road, and we follow this track northwest toward a bald, unnamed 8800-foot prominence that is sometimes used for a fire lookout. Along this segment, a dirt road to Underwood Valley departs to the right, uphill, in the middle of a vast field of mule ears. Curving around the west side of that prominence, our trail enters the Mokelumne Wilderness at the divide between the Mokelumne River and the Stanislaus River.

Here begins the 3500-foot, almost unrelieved descent. Fortunately for those coming back up, there is water at several places in all but the driest years. From the wilderness boundary our steeply descending, rubbly trail passes close under some dark, clifflike volcanic outcroppings from which boulders have broken off and rolled down to the trail and beyond. The path then switchbacks down to approach the stream in Lake Valley,

Lake Valley

passing a fair campsite before veering more northward and
leaving this stream. The Mokelumne River, thousands of feet
below, is a slim silver thread where it is visible between mask-
ing stands of trees. The only partly shaded descent remains
gentle, almost a contour, down to the 7200-foot level, and
then begin more switchbacks, which characterize most of the
rest of the descent to Camp Irene. A series of flower gardens—
in season—brighten the canyonside as the trail more or less
parallels the Underwood Valley stream for almost a mile of
northward descent. Finally, at about 5600 feet elevation, the
gradient abates considerably and the trail heads northwest
toward Camp Irene, which is reached from Silver Lake by Secs.
1.6, 1.10 and 2.17. There are good pools for swimming here,
although the water is far from steamy, and fishermen will find
that some large brown trout have spells of rising to the fly.

Log at Camp Irene

Sec. 3.4 Camp Irene to Salt Springs Reservoir (trailway: 15 miles)

What was a formidable cross-country route from Camp Irene to Cedar Camp and an unspeakably uncivilized route from there downstream, has become, thanks to our friends in the Forest Service, a ducked-and-blazed trailway, relatively easy to follow, all the way to Salt Springs Reservoir. Make no mistake: this is no place for your arthritic grandmother. It is still tough going—plenty of loops up and away from the river and then steeply back down again, sometimes over rock, sometimes through brush, and plenty of opportunity to lose your way from time to time. But no longer does it consume your physical and mental energies to the point of obscuring enjoyment—and there is plenty of that, too. The scenery in this part of the river canyon is ever-changing, from cataracts to quiet pools, from firs to cedars to oaks, from close granite walls to marvelously towering peaks, and there are dozens of places where you can camp alone.

Describing the route is difficult because of the constant changes in direction, elevation and terrain. Basically, it consists of a series of arcs away from the river and back again, gaining elevation each time and then dropping back. For the first 1/3 mile the route lies close to the north bank of the river. Then it makes a semiloop, passing through a kind of notch between the granite walls on the north side of the canyon and a lateral ridge that runs north-south between the granite walls and the river. Dropping back to the river again, the route follows it closely for ½ mile through a forest of lodgepole pine, incense-cedar and alder to Cedar Camp. Less crowded than Camp Irene, it has good camping plus the bonus of fine swimming in a large hole just downstream.

From Cedar Camp the route follows close to the river for about 1 mile, passing near some large pools, and then makes two more arcs in succession. The first of these takes you several hundred feet above the river in a fairly direct route southwest (while the riverbed bulges in an arc to the southeast), and brings you back down to a parklike setting where the river flows through flat, lazy pools. There follows a short second arc, returning to the river at a good campsite.

For about 1½ miles thereafter, the route follows within 200 yards of the river; then there is a succession of arcs as the route traverses the base of the towering Mokelumne Tetons to the north. This is a spectacular stretch, and particularly beautiful in early or late light. There are some falls along the river along the way—you have to be alert to catch them—and a number of beautiful, granite-lined pools, a few with sandy beaches.

After 1½ more miles of upping and downing, the route arrives at Blue Hole (not all that blue, but at the bottom of a particularly beautiful stretch of the river), and in another ½ mile at the reservoir. The trail around the north side of the reservoir to the dam—about 4½ miles—is about as dull as most reservoir trails, but at least it is fairly easy going, and there are opportunities for dips along the way. From the dam (where we hope you have left your car or have arranged to be met) a road winds 14 miles up to the abandoned ranger station at Lumberyard on Highway 88. Check at the ranger station for directions before you or your friend drives down.

Sec. 3.5 Hermit Valley to Summit City Creek
(cross country, 10 miles)

(This route starts east of our map, in the *Markleeville* quadrangle.) From a parking lot on the north side of Highway 4 at Hermit Valley, just east of where the highway crosses the Mokelumne River, a rugged route leads down the north side of the river to Summit City Creek. From time to time the Forest Service has marked the route with ribbons, but most of these have been removed by fisherfolk determined to preserve their favorite holes, and perhaps that is just as well. The route is not easy to follow, but it presents a fine challenge to those with cross-country experience and a spirit of adventure who do not mind getting their faces and limbs scratched and perhaps their packs wet.

The route starts out in a deceptively easy manner, descending to the river on a moderate traverse and a series of switchbacks, but then any semblance of a civilized trail soon disappears. After crossing a boulder-filled dry wash and then a stream which shows on the map as seasonal but which was quite full in late October, the route enters the Mokelumne Wilderness and makes a seemingly endless series of loops up, away from the river and then back, down to the river, over granite, through brush, in generally trying fashion. The route enters this book's map ¾ mile west of the wilderness boundary. The canyon begins to open out at Meadow Creek, and from here on to Summit City Creek it is, except for the effort, sheer delight. Many fine camp spots lie along the way.

Section 4   Trails from Lower Bear River Reservoir

About the only good thing that can be said concerning Lower Bear River Reservoir and Salt Springs Reservoir, from the point of view of the hiker and backpacker, is that the road construction associated with them made parts of the wilderness more accessible. Concededly that is a mixed blessing, but as long as it's given, you might as well take advantage of it.

Sec. 4.1   Tanglefoot Trailhead to Shriner Lake (2 miles)

The trail to Shriner Lake from the Tanglefoot Trailhead has been described, in the opposite direction, in section 1.12. The trailhead is located in a heavily logged area, and may at times be difficult to locate. The road to Lower Bear River Reservoir leads south from Highway 88 near Peddler Hill and crosses the spillway on the reservoir's south shore. Where the pavement ends, the road forks. Keep left at that fork, then follow the signs for Cole Creek at subsequent forks. After crossing Cole Creek on a recently constructed bridge, bear right, following the signs to *Tanglefoot Trail*.

Sec. 4.2   Cole Creek Trail

As the road from Lower Bear River Reservoir approaches Cole Creek, it makes a sharp U turn, and at the apex of the turn a route heads east up the north side of Cole Creek. A jeep road at first, this route becomes more trail-like after ½ mile. By the end of the second mile, the trail is deep in Cole Creek Canyon, with steep granite walls on both sides. Here there are splendid pools for swimming and fishing. The trail becomes undulating as the terrain becomes more uneven, and finally, by the end of the third mile, the trail begins to head north out of the canyon to meet a stream that flows out of Willow Flat. Here the trail becomes increasingly indistinct (Sec. 4.3). It is possible, however, to follow Cole Creek upstream through the canyon for another mile or so, and many fishermen have done so.

Sec. 4.3 Upper Pardoes Camp to Cole Creek

Maps show a trail beginning at Upper Pardoes Camp and heading southeast to meet the trail up Cole Creek. No doubt such a trail once existed, but it doesn't now, at least in the upper part. To get from Upper Pardoes Camp to the Cole Creek Trail, it is necessary to head cross-country east from Upper Pardoes Camp, descending moderately to steeply until you meet the stream out of Willow Flat, about halfway down. Here, if you look hard, you will find old blazes and the remnants of a trail. The trail crosses the stream, then recrosses and descends steeply south to Cole Creek Canyon.

Round Top Lake

Index

Conservation organizations

The price of wilderness, like liberty, is eternal vigilance. Someone is always about to carve off a piece of wilderness to use for tree cutting, mining, ski resorts or something else. If you always want to have nice places to go backpacking, you'll have to expend a little effort to help save these places. Fortunately, there are a number of existing organizations that are already set up to work for wilderness. They simply need your help.

I urge you to get in touch with any or all of the organizations listed below, and join the ones that seem best to you.

Appalachian Mountain Club
5 Joy St.
Boston, MA 02108

American Hiking Society
1701 18th St. N.W.
Washington, D.C. 20009

California Wilderness
    Coalition
2655 Portage Bay Ave.
Suite 3
Davis, CA 95616

The Mountaineers
300 3rd Ave. W.
Seattle, WA 98119

National Parks and
    Conservation Association
1701 18th St. N.W.
Washington, D.C. 20009

Sierra Club
730 Polk St.
San Francisco, CA 94109

The Wilderness Society
1400 Eye St. N.W.
Washington, D.C. 20005

—Thomas Winnett, President
Wilderness Press

Acknowledgements

Many people have been helpful along the way. We particularly want to thank Monroe "Spud" DeJarnette, Eric Burr and Woody Hesselbarth, who are or have been wilderness rangers in Eldorado National Forest, and whose knowledge of both trails and cross-country routes is unsurpassed. We have been inspired by walks and talks with Jess Machado, who has been coming to Silver Lake longer than anyone but he can remember, and whose understanding of and appreciation for this region and its history are truly extraordinary. Dean Taylor, botanist, has supplemented our meager knowledge of flora; and Clyde Wahrhaftig, geologist, has supplied most of the material for that section of the book. Finally, to my wife, Janet, and our daughter, Lisa, who walked many of the trails, provided innumerable shuttles, and displayed admirable patience throughout, our gratitude and love.

—Joseph R. Grodin
Berkeley, California
February 15, 1990

Outdoor Book Specialists

Wilderness Press has over 70 accurate, high-quality books and maps now in print containing all the information you need to enjoy a trip to the utmost.

We've been there—from the High Sierra to the Hawaiian Islands, from Arizona to Minnesota. We've covered Yosemite, Lassen, Crater Lake, Sequoia, Kings Canyon, and more.

Books for outdoor adventurers, both active and armchair.

Ask your dealer to show you the other Wilderness Press books and maps he stocks. Or write for our free mail-order catalog.

WILDERNESS PRESS
2440M Bancroft Way
Berkeley, CA 94704